THE PROPERTY MANAGER'S HANDBOOK:

Business Planning for the Professional

Stephen G. Pappas, CPM

Real Estate Education Company
a division of Dearborn Financial Publishing, Inc.

While a great deal of care has been taken to provide accurate and current information, the ideas, suggestions, general principles and conclusions presented in this book are subject to local, state and federal laws and regulations, court cases and any revisions of same. The reader is thus urged to consult legal counsel regarding any points of law—this publication should not be used as a substitute for competent legal advice.

Publisher: Kathleen A. Welton
Acquisitions Editor: Patrick Hogan
Associate Editor: Karen A. Christensen
Senior Project Editor: Jack L. Kiburz

Published by Real Estate Education Company,
a division of Dearborn Financial Publishing, Inc.

Printed in the United States of America

91 92 93 10 9 8 7 6 5 4 3 2 1

Library of Congress Cataloging-in-Publication Data

Pappas, Stephen G., 1939–
　　The property manager's handbook : business planning for the professional / by Stephen G. Pappas.
　　　　p.　cm.
　　Includes index.
　　ISBN 0-79310-214-6 (case)
　　1. Real estate management. I. Title.
HD1394P37　1991　　　　　　　　　　　　　　　　90-26155
647′.068—dc20　　　　　　　　　　　　　　　　　　　CIP

Dedication

To my wife, Irene, and my children, Athena, Denyse, and Elaine

Contents

Preface

It is a truism that knowledge and experience are necessary to recognizing opportunity. But I had often wondered what triggers the recognition process, the moment of "Eureka!" that Archimedes noted in his discovery of specific gravity over two millennia ago.

In the case of this book, the moment came when a young colleague of mine asked me to recommend a book about operating a property management company. As is true of most people in the field for a number of years, my vision had been narrowed by the business demands of my own specialty. I asked my colleague what types of properties he was considering.

He insisted that it didn't matter, and after a few minutes of discussion I began to understand what he wanted—a book not on managing properties, but on managing the property management business itself.

I couldn't think of any, but was willing to chalk it up to ignorance. A few days later, I found myself in a local bookstore, browsing through the business and economics section for my colleague's book. I could find none.

Now more than a little curious, I had an associate perform a computerized search of books through one of the databases on the Dialog information system. His search of all books published in the United States by 22,000 publishers since 1979 indicated some 244 books dealing with managing companies. None, however, specifically addressed the subject of managing property management businesses.

To be sure, a few property management books did broach the subject of office management in individual chapters that amounted to about 5 percent of the books' total content. However, there appeared to be no single, comprehensive book on operating the business as a business.

The proverbial light bulb went on in my head, and the book you are now holding in your hand is a result of that moment of recognition.

The Property Manager's Handbook does not dwell on matters of everyday property management except as they affect the management business itself. It is designed as a reference source for owners of both new and existing property management firms and, in this regard, it discusses *property* as opposed to *asset* management. However, asset management organizations—which deal more with the needs of corporate and institutional concerns—will be able to benefit as well.

This handbook's concise format is designed to guide the professional in making quick and effective decisions in the operation of the business as well as aid property owners in better understanding the business of professional property management.

Obviously, not every topic in this book will apply to every property management business, and owners/managers with varying degrees of experience will find some chapters more useful than others. However, all should benefit through the comprehension of policies, plans and procedures created to effectively manage what is, in the final analysis, an investment in one's life.

Professional property management firms bring a special service to our society by going beyond the creation and/or maintenance of beautiful and harmonious properties in the community. The existence of these firms makes the statement that the future is important and that what we build and maintain today is the key to that future.

I hope this book will add to the existing knowledge about property management in a way that invites you to learn and, in so doing, help point the way.

Stephen G. Pappas, CPM

Acknowledgments

I am happy to acknowledge the time, energy and expertise of attorney Jerome Skyrud of Phoenix, Arizona, Joe Binsfeld, C.I.C., vice president of ISU/General Southwest Insurance Agency, Phoenix, and Janet Hanson, C.P.A., partner, Hanson and Raskin, Phoenix.

Thanks also must go to Phil Harrison, who kept a very complex and evolving manuscript on target.

S.G.P.

1: A Perspective on the Property Management Business

Although property management as a profession has come into its own only since the end of World War II, its beginnings can be traced to the growth of modern cities, particularly with the development of the skyscraper. Around the turn of the century, the typical financial arrangement for such a building involved leasing the land, rather than buying it, and obtaining construction funds through stock and bond issues. This created the tradition of multiownership of income properties, a relative rarity beforehand.

Additionally, because skyscrapers were so new, many of them began to fail economically because of design defects and extravagances that seriously affected their earning power. Around 1915, these related events elevated a previously unimportant part of real estate—leasing office space—into a new professional specialty.

As the skyscraper was the catalyst for property management, the automobile was the means through which suburban life, as we know it today, became possible, and property values soared. The railroads added $30 billion to U.S. land values by the turn of the 20th century. It was estimated that the automobile would increase that figure more than threefold. As land values increased, the need to better protect properties to ensure their economic viability increased as well.

However, the real boom for professional property managers began with the end of World War II, and the rise of large financial institutions, industries, labor unions, shopping centers and governments. The sheer size of these entities—and the cost of projects being created—required a new approach to management; hence such 1950s concepts as strategic planning, methods analysis and management by objectives.

Such thought, especially management by objectives, permeated the property management industry, which had grown considerably but had remained strictly task-oriented. Property managers were concerned with renting and leasing, for example, rather than marketing, with cutting costs rather than planning for the long haul, with accounting statements rather than accounting analysis.

It's true that cutting costs and preparing good accounting statements are important tasks, but the exclusive adherence to these tasks changed in the late Sixties and early Seventies when the real estate industry received its greatest financial outlay for new development. This outlay was created in great part by involving the public through limited partnerships and real estate investment trusts (REITs). As a result, the size of a typical office building quadrupled from its Fifties predecessor, apartment buildings grew from 25 or 50 units to 100 or even 500 units and shopping centers developed into regional malls.

People began to realize that managing such properties in this rapidly expanding environment would require a focus on opportunities rather than specific problems. The modern property manager had arrived.

UNDERSTANDING THE REQUIREMENTS OF
PROPERTY MANAGEMENT

In order to understand the operation of a property management firm, it is necessary to answer three questions:

1. Why is there a need for a property management firm?

2. What does a property management firm do?

3. What different types of management services can be provided?

As mentioned previously, the need for property management has never been greater. Yet, while its overall responsibility is to protect the value of a property, the management firm is typically the last to be hired in the chain of real estate development. The scenario for an average real estate project illustrates this statement.

A consultant first reviews the owner's needs and wants. A real estate broker locates the site. A lawyer reviews the sales contract. A mortgage company provides the funds. An architect designs the structure. An engineer handles the particulars of off-site and on-site mechanical and electrical design, while a heating and air-conditioning specialist makes recommendations for year-round climate control.

Then a project manager coordinates the construction of the entire project, while a contractor actually builds the building. Proper insurance coverage, of course, has already been put in place.

A landscape architect designs the surrounding land for beauty and practicality. An interior designer becomes responsible for tenant improvements, a telephone specialist puts a communications system into operation and a leasing agent is then hired to market the entire project.

Finally, a property management firm is hired to deal with the problems left by everyone else. Logic would seem to dictate that a management firm be brought into the process from the very beginning in order to avoid possible problems and thus add to the efficiency and value of the project.

This having been noted, a property management firm, in general:

- protects the value of the property,
- provides timely reports to the owners,
- has knowledge of both local and national trends in the property management business,
- complies with established policies and procedures and
- instills confidence that the overall management of the property is being performed correctly.

Three types of service can accomplish these goals to varying degrees:

1. **Asset management.** Asset management assumes complete responsibility for the economic prosperity of a property and provides all necessary accounting and reporting. It is also concerned with the funds available beyond the net operating income and how to either invest them effectively in the property or provide for a distribution to the owners.
2. **Property management.** This type of management handles the maintenance, leasing, accounting and reporting functions as indicated solely by net operating income. The owner often has the final word on the use of these funds, policies developed and, sometimes, employees hired.
3. **Supervisory management.** This is concerned only with trouble-shooting or consulting, either for owners or for other property management firms (usually out of state). Financial reporting is done by another organization or by the owner.

Regardless of whether you decide to provide one, two or all three types of service, the basic management skills are identical. That is, you must be able to demonstrate that

- your company has a professional organizational structure with clearly defined and proven policies;

- your company's principals not only have the knowledge of property management, but also the practical experience necessary to manage a particular type of property;
- your company has specific procedures to address such situations as property takeover, employee and on-site training, maintenance and emergencies;
- your company understands the importance of, and is capable of properly administering, all reporting and accounting functions; and
- your company has proper insurance in force.

All of these items will be discussed in the chapters ahead.

Within these parameters are three different levels of management, each with a viewpoint to fulfill.

The *management firm* is responsible for the entire operation of the property within contractual/service boundaries. On occasion, it also acts as a consultant, broker, appraiser and/or developer.

The *property manager* handles the overall operation of the property and is directly responsible to the management firm. It is not unusual for such a manager to be involved in the operation of several properties.

This person's goal is total efficiency. He or she needs a good understanding of economics, marketing and law in order to perform such varied tasks as purchasing equipment, hiring and firing personnel, inspecting property, enforcing leases, collecting rents, developing budgets, surveying the market, marketing and leasing as well as planning for the future. And the property manager must always act in the interest of the property owner(s), while maintaining good relations with the tenants.

The *resident manager* usually works (or lives) on the premises and deals directly with tenants, with whom he or she must establish a good rapport. Duties include showing space to prospective tenants, collecting rent, performing or arranging for the required maintenance, keeping the books and perhaps even developing social programs.

To be sure, a management firm often includes other employees such as a comptroller, a receptionist and secretaries. (A discussion of these employees can be found in Chapter 4.)

AN OVERVIEW OF BASIC MANAGEMENT FIRM RESPONSIBILITIES

All property management firms have three major objectives and responsibilities. In order of importance, they are (1) to relieve the owner/investor of the day-to-day burdens of operation and management; (2) to establish operational efficiencies and economies that will reflect maximum income potential for the owner and (3) to demonstrate to tenants and the community a level of professional property control.

To meet these objectives, management companies must make an agreement with the property owner before taking on a new project. This management agreement is essentially a written understanding that covers in detail what each party expects of the other. (A sample management contract appears in Appendix D.)

In general, a management agreement is an employment contract. It establishes the owner's relationship to the company and transfers managerial power of attorney to the managers. It spells out the rights, responsibilities and limitations of managers so as to avoid misunderstandings. It states the terms of compensation that will be paid for management services and provides for termination of services.

In addition to managing all personnel and real property as described in the contract, the management firm usually reviews annually all insurance coverage to determine if it is adequate and economical, requires valid copies of worker's compensation and liability coverage for all contractors before they undertake work on the property, supplies 24-hour emergency phone service, arranges for an annual audit (uncertified) and preparation of federal and state returns by an outside accounting firm, processes all payroll and files all quarterly reports, works with the accountant and prepares all forms, reports and returns required by the law as it relates to the employees.

The firms also obtains contracts for all utilities, extermination and lawn service, major pool repairs, painting, common area insurance and other such services as may be necessary. In addition, it arranges for the completion of takeover and termination procedures on properties, confers with owners on all important matters as well as maintains businesslike relations with all owners.

This sounds like a lot of work, and it is. Figure 1.1 illustrates these responsibilities more simply.

In general, there are four steps:

1. **Develop a plan.** Prepare a management plan, approved by the owners, that will guide the operation of the property.
2. **Provide services.** All necessary services must be done either by company personnel or through subcontracting.
3. **Communicate regularly.** All activities of the property must be communicated to the owner(s) through either financial report, written narrative or oral presentation.
4. **Establish activity centers.** These centers will make it easier to plan for and maintain such services as managing the property,

Figure 1.1   Management Company Responsibilities

```
┌──────────────────┐          ┌──────────────────┐
│ INVESTOR/OWNER   │          │   MANAGEMENT     │
│ Seeks fair return├──────────┤    COMPANY       │
│ on investment    │          │                  │
└──────────────────┘          └──────────────────┘
                                       │
                              ┌──────────────────┐
                              │    DEVELOPS       │
                              │       A           │
                              │      PLAN         │
                              └──────────────────┘
                                       │
                              ┌──────────────────┐
                              │    PROVIDES       │
                              │    SERVICES       │
                              └──────────────────┘
                                       │
                              ┌──────────────────┐
                              │  COMMUNICATIONS   │
                              └──────────────────┘
                                       │
  ┌─────────┬──────────┬──────────┬──────────┬──────────┐
┌────────┐┌──────────┐┌──────────┐┌─────────┐┌──────────┐
│PROPERTY││ACCOUNTING││ OFFICE/  ││MARKETING││  OTHER   │
│MANAGE- ││REPORTING ││SECRETARY ││         ││ SERVICES │
│MENT    ││          ││OPERATION ││         ││          │
└────────┘└──────────┘└──────────┘└─────────┘└──────────┘
```

accounting for the money, administering office procedures, marketing, consulting, renovating and so forth.

   A good property management firm must be able to make a property "work" in accordance with the owner's buying or development decision. To accomplish this goal, your firm must be a combination of good citizen, lawyer, appraiser, economist, architect or space planner, broker, public relations expert, building maintenance expert and psychologist. This last role is among the most important in dealing with the people (and other businesses) and getting to know their abilities and idiosyncrasies.

   Beyond this, the next most important aspect of good management (and, conversely, the next most likely cause of failure) is keeping an extensive set of good records. As a general rule, owners who do not also manage their properties keep notoriously poor records. Therefore, a major responsibility of the newly hired property management firm is to correct this fault.

   In accomplishing this task, a property management firm must take three basic steps:

1. **Set up the property on files.** A systematic approach to this is essential (see Chapter 4).
2. **Inspect the property.** A property inspection report is used to develop a comprehensive look at the property to determine its physical status.
3. **Develop a management plan.** This written document is designed for review by the owner, who will recommend a management direction.

It is essential that a property management firm be able to understand the owner's objectives and formulate a long-range plan that is consistent with them. In this respect, the management firm must learn the owner's attitudes and goals during initial meetings. Otherwise, differences in philosophies will create friction in the later operation of the property.

In general, a property management company should have a plan for each property to be managed. Although specifics will vary from company to company, a generic outline of a long-range management plan might look like the following:

  I. Market Analysis
      A. Regional
      B. Neighborhood

 II. Property Analysis
      A. Physical
      B. Fiscal
      C. Operational
          1. Policies and procedures
          2. Employees

III. Analysis of Alternate Management Programs

 IV. Recommendations
      A. Staff
      B. Operating procedures
      C. Physical changes
      D. Cost estimates

  V. Timetables for Implementation

To implement the plan, a property management firm must initially have all the details about the property, including (but not limited to) the

- size of the property;
- total number of units/square feet;
- size of all structures on the property;
- all tenants' names, addresses and phone numbers;
- copies of all leases, contracts and other legal documents;
- detailed rent roll;
- past expense statements;
- all purchasing data and details of financing;
- complete payroll and employee data;
- maintenance records; and
- all insurance policies.

If the owner does not have this information, arrangements should be made to secure it. The New Account Management Takeover and Checklist (Figure 1.2) will help tremendously in this regard.

The neighborhood and regional analyses noted in the outline above are marketing reports designed to help determine the property's current position in the overall scheme of things and the possible need for change. What you will need to answer here are questions about the appropriateness of the property's target market, promotional materials, lease terms, anticipated lease-up, and projections and strategy for renewals.

The Property Inspection Report will help determine the physical needs (if any) of the property. The Tenant/Occupancy Profile and Marketing Checklist will help in determining the existing tenant makeup. The Competitive Property Rent Analysis represents a good starting point for understanding competing properties. Copies of these forms can be found in Appendix D.

Once these initial items have been developed to everyone's satisfaction and the management plan has been approved, it will be possible to begin everyday property management and operation.

THE FUTURE OF PROPERTY MANAGEMENT

Even though a major characteristic of the real estate industry is its cyclical nature, many owners and developers tend to assume that everything will remain the same. This attitude is chiefly responsible for mediocre development performance and low market acceptance. To paraphrase an old saying, the best property manager in the world will not be able to get blood from a stone.

It is unlikely that this cyclicality will disappear, however, without dramatic changes to the economic structure of the country, much as occurred during the Depression and immediately following World War II.

Figure 1.2   New Account Management Takeover and Checklist

Property: _____ Date: _____

Prepared By: _____

GENERAL INFORMATION

Address: _____

Telephone Number: _____

Legal Description and Lot/Parcel Number: _____

_____

_____

Investor/Representative: _____
    Address: _____
    Telephone Number: _____
    Monthly Report To: _____
    Copies To: _____

Management Contract Date Signed: _____ Effective: _____

Previous Owner: _____

Previous Managing Agent: _____

Insurance Policies In File: Property _____, Liability _____,
    Auto _____, Crime _____, Worker's Compensation _____,
    Others _____
    Management Department Insured Endorsement In File: _____

Gross Sq. Ft. _____, Net Sq. Ft. _____

Land Size: _____ Acres, _____ Sq. Ft., Front Footage: _____

Improvements (Site Amenities): _____

_____

_____

_____

Purchase Price: _____ Purchase Date: _____ Down Payment: _____

Assessed Value Of Building: _____, Assessed Value Of Land: _____

Tax Bill:
    Amount: _____, Months Due: _____
    Paid By: Owner _____, Escrow Monthly _____, Other _____

First Mortgage Information:
    Paid To: _____
    Current Mortgage Balance Due: $_____
    Loan Terms: _____ years, _____ % interest
    Monthly Payments: $ _____. Includes: Taxes _____, Insurance _____, Others _____

Second Mortgage Information:
    Paid To: _____
    Current Mortgage Balance Due $ _____
    Loan Terms: _____ years, _____ % interest
    Monthly Payments: $ _____. Includes: Taxes _____, Insurance _____, Others _____

Figure 1.2 (Continued)   Property Information

	Initials*	Date Completed
GENERAL		
(a) Obtain operating budgets for preceding year and current year	_____	_____
(b) Local and state Landlord/Tenant Laws	_____	_____
(c) Transfer titles where necessary	_____	_____
(d) Rental agreement/rules and reg./policies	_____	_____
(e) Order project forms	_____	_____
(f) Assign project manuals	_____	_____
(g) Personnel training	_____	_____
(h) Project policies	_____	_____
(i) Post labor information for employees	_____	_____
(j) Send form letter to tenants on takeover	_____	_____
(k) Insurance policy changeover information	_____	_____
(l) Keys and pertinent files received	_____	_____
(m) Convert record-keeping system and forms to our system	_____	_____
(n) Acquire copies and review all contracts with vendors/contractors currently in force	_____	_____
(o) Send letters to vendors stating our insurance requirements and requesting certificates of insurance	_____	_____
(p) Set of "as built" plans, photographs	_____	_____
(q) List deferred maintenance	_____	_____
(r) Review project security	_____	_____
(s) List any pending litigation	_____	_____
(t) Warranties on all mechanical equipment	_____	_____
(u) Market study	_____	_____
(v) Fill-up projections	_____	_____
(w) Rent increase projections	_____	_____
(x) Marketing program	_____	_____
(y) Membership in Chamber of Commerce, etc.	_____	_____
(z) Business/State/City/County licenses	_____	_____
(@) Health permits/use permits	_____	_____
(#) Obtain all necessary correspondence	_____	_____
RESIDENTIAL		
(a) Total number of units	_____	_____
(b) Unit sizes, rates and types (studios, 1 bdrm)	_____	_____
(c) Public utility deposits—bond information	_____	_____
(d) Unit amenities—inventory	_____	_____
(e) Project inventory	_____	_____
(f) Initial tenant roster with copy of lease	_____	_____
(g) Detailed list of deposits and prepaid rent	_____	_____
COMMERCIAL		
(a) Set up tenant roster	_____	_____
(b) Make Space-Available Sheet for building	_____	_____
(c) Inventory of leasehold improvement materials and supplies	_____	_____
CONDO/TOWNHOUSE		
(a) Minutes of meetings	_____	_____
(b) Liens and releases	_____	_____
(c) Bylaws, CC & R, articles, rules & reg.	_____	_____
(d) Lot files	_____	_____

*Responsible party to sign and date.

Figure 1.2 (Continued)   Financial Information

	Initials*	Date Completed
INCOME		
(a) Names of all lessees (Tenant Master File)	————	————
Unit sizes (square footage)	————	————
Monthly rental	————	————
Rental due dates	————	————
Current list of delinquencies	————	————
(b) List of current vacancies	————	————
(c) List of current leases on notice	————	————
(d) Prospective tenant list	————	————
(e) Set up ledger cards/computer	————	————
(f) Other income	————	————
(g) Gross sales reports for tenants for past year	————	————
OPERATING EXPENSE		
(a) Copy of current and all past tax bills	————	————
(b) Copies of most recent licenses and other tax bills	————	————
(c) List of all outstanding bills on hand	————	————
(d) Copies of most recent annual operating statements	————	————
(e) Copies of tenant escalation bills	————	————
(f) Establish supplier list	————	————
COMMON AREA EXPENSE (Expenses being billed back to tenants)		
(a) Salaries, payroll taxes, etc.	————	————
(b) Office expenses	————	————
(c) Vehicle/mileage allowance	————	————
(d) Original copies of all agreements with each contractor, service company and supplier	————	————
PAYROLL		
(a) Prepare employee envelope-file	————	————
(b) Set up time card procedures on-site if applicable (first day)	————	————
ACCOUNTING		
(a) Assign project number	————	————
(b) Set up bank account	————	————
(c) Prepare bank cards, signatures	————	————
(d) Order checks, deposit slips, endorsement stamps	————	————
(e) Set up management fee information	————	————
(f) Establish type of operating statement owner requests	————	————
(g) List of security deposits being held, show how held (cash, savings account, etc.)	————	————
(h) Loan payment information set-up	————	————
(i) Set up supplier list	————	————
(j) Tax returns	————	————
(k) Audit reports	————	————

*Responsible party to sign and date.

Although it is possible that recent events in Europe and along the Pacific Rim may yield dramatic changes, astute property managers must still envision the users of tomorrow in order to understand the future role of the industry.

The physical and institutional forms of the suburbs as we know them today, for example, were largely shaped by the 20-year baby boom following World War II (Figure 1.3). As a result, the age composition of urban centers changed. Coupled with the decline in the birthrate, the population of central urban areas has been declining, urban renewal programs notwithstanding.

But many suburbs, their formative growth having occurred in the Fifties and Sixties, are currently being underutilized. The original owners, for example, may still live there but their baby-boom children have left. This has resulted in elderly couples or single people living in houses designed for large families—at a time when many young people are having trouble becoming homeowners.

All manner of public and private services (e.g., schools, churches, retail centers) have had to adapt themselves to these conditions, and they have not always been successful. This situation will continue and present great challenges in the beginning decades of the 21st century.

It is also likely that, despite the so-called gentrification trend of the inner cities, the movement of people to the suburbs will continue. Interestingly, however, the slowdown in family formation coupled with the rising cost of single-family homes has produced a new need for multifamily and apartment construction in the suburbs—one of the reasons that people originally left the cities in the Fifties!

The baby boomers, 78 million people or one-third of the total population of the country, will continue to determine the direction of real estate and, as their needs change through the aging process, so will the need for property management expertise. We can divide this expertise into four areas: retail, hospitality, housing and the workplace.

Retail

Counting the baby boomers' entry into middle-age, close to 40 percent of the population is entering what are traditionally the peak earning years. As such, we can expect retail purchases to increase, supporting new shopping malls and allowing for the renovation of old ones.

Over the last decade, we have seen many malls become mixed-use centers incorporating office buildings and hotels. We can expect this trend to continue and expand. However, because of the large number of mature, working adults with limited time for shopping, malls will eventually become "town centers." They will include small museums and amusement

**Figure 1.3   U.S. Birthrate
(per thousand population)**

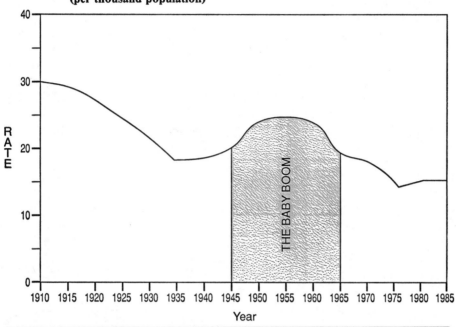

SOURCE: Department of Health and Human Services

centers, in addition to the health club, day-care facilities and medical clinics that are already locating there.

More retail centers will also be staying open longer hours (some 24 hours a day) and in order to remain competitive, they will offer special services and evening events. This competition will come not only from other malls, but from an increasing use of direct marketing (i.e., mail, television and telephone sales).

Hospitality

Two seemingly disparate events will dominate change in this industry: the aging of the population and the presence of children.

People over 50 already dominate the pleasure travel and tourism business, and we can expect many lodging and resort facilities to shift their orientation to serve this growing market in the coming decades. We can expect an increasing need for health facilities (i.e., spas) and packaged experiences, such as trips with scientists to view solar eclipses, assist in actual archeological digs, etc.

Similarly, propelled by demand from the maturing baby-boom generation, segments of this industry that once merely tolerated traveling families are beginning to see the profit in making them feel welcome. Some business and luxury hotels are already adding day-care programs and day camps.

In the future, we can expect to see "miniclub" resorts providing day camps, baby-sitting and escorted trips to museums or the zoo (with a pediatrician on call around the clock). Also expect children to have their own rooms, connected to their parents' rooms, at a discount rate.

Housing

Because of the increasing number of nontraditional households, we can expect demand to grow for new housing products: rental retirement and congregate care communities, nursing homes, condominiumlike developments for empty nesters, townhouses for childless households, vacation homes, and developments especially designed for single parents and families in which both parents work.

In the case of the last group and empty nesters, the most successful developments will be near transportation nodes close to services, entertainment and employment centers.

We can also expect that the market for owning a second home will expand, particularly with a maturing population entering its peak earning cycle.

Traditional rental housing may be in for highly competitive times, especially since some 50 percent of its market—singles under 34 years old—will drop significantly by the year 2000. Property managers may be able to offset this trend by appealing to what will be an increasing number of middle-aged adults without children, a group that also tends to favor such housing.

The Workplace

The aging of the population also means an eventual decline in the traditional workforce. In 1986, for example, the number of workers aged 16–19 was 20 percent lower than it was in 1978. This decrease will continue at least through the late 1990s.

Businesses that traditionally depend on young, low-waged workers (e.g., hospitality, tourism, food service) have experienced this shrinking labor force, with resulting higher operating costs. All other industries will feel it within the next decade.

The effects of this shrinking labor force on real estate will be varied, but we can be sure that a slowing growth in employment translates into reduced demand for office space. However, the consequent increased competition for employees will place a premium on amenities in the workplace. Thus, we can anticipate the inclusion of health, educational, recreational, entertainment and day-care facilities on-site.

Specifically, on-site day-care centers may become commonplace in the coming decades. In some areas of the country, business park developers are already using day-care facilities to appeal to prospective corporate tenants. Large chains of independent day-care centers have also sprung up across the country, many entering the corporate marketplace.

The pressure for such facilities will be felt most particularly in the South and West, where the number of young children is growing fastest.

2: Ethics, Laws and Liabilities

A requirement of the property management business is that its practitioners maintain high ethical and professional standards. Most managers understand (or should understand) what is meant by professional standards, which generally involve matters of competency and proficiency. But what do we mean when we talk of ethics? The answer to this question is important in appreciating both the requirements of law and the subsequent need for liability or insurance coverage.

Technically, *ethics* is defined as a system of moral principles or rules of conduct. We might elaborate on that to include integrity, responsibility and trust (all of which are vital to the truly successful management operation). The problem with choosing any words in a definition is that ethics is essentially a social and cultural, rather than a legal, phenomenon and, as such, is not identical for all people at all times. That many appear concerned with issues of ethics—in this case, the manner in which business is conducted—indicates an American interpretation of fairness—everyone playing by the same set of rules (an ethic in itself).

The purpose of law, therefore, is to define formally certain standards of ethical behavior. Understand the law of a society and you in theory understand the ethical principles that guide it.

To be sure, most property managers are aware of their ethical responsibilities to their business and their obligations not only to the industry and the people who provide capital, but also to employees, clients, tenants, suppliers, government and competitors. However, as many ethical responsibilities are not written into law, managers must be more than aware of these considerations. They must teach their employees, instilling ethical values in those who, after all, have direct (and often first) contact with clients and others in business. Property managers must codify in policies and rules what the company considers to be an appropriate standard of business conduct in various situations. Most major real estate trade organizations have developed codes of professional ethics. Whether you choose to abide by one of them or develop your own, it must be in writing and all of your employees and clients must have a copy and understand the meaning of all provisions.

This having been said, however, there are some ethical considerations in the form of law—and regulations that have the effect of law—that influence the operation of a property management business. For managers, these laws can be divided into two questions for practical consideration:

1. *How does the law affect the way in which I can operate my business?*

2. *How can I fulfill the law's requirements on a daily basis?*

Unfortunately, no single book can answer these questions. The Bill of Rights and the U.S. Constitution form the basis of all law in the United States. Nevertheless, most laws that govern the use of real estate come from many sources, including Congress, state constitutions, state and local legislatures (and bureaucracies), court interpretations, and what is referred to as common law. This can be seen more clearly as we arrange the types of laws that affect the property management business under the headings of either national or state (local):

National
- Environmental laws
- Fair housing laws
- Gas pipe corrosion laws
- Occupational safety and health laws
- Minimum wage laws
- Income and social security taxes
- Urban renewal

State (Local)
- Energy conservation and environmental laws
- Fair housing laws and housing programs
- Contract laws
- Landlord/tenant laws
- Personal property tax laws
- Real estate tax laws
- Income tax laws
- Rent control

- Zoning/development/building codes: Building and manufacturing codes, health and safety, land use and no or limited growth policies
- Operational: Business licenses, employment laws, real estate license laws, permits and guest registration

Fortunately, because the Bill of Rights and the Constitution are the basis for all law, there are similarities in local laws. Although the following listing is by no means complete, it is basic to describing the legal responsibilities for operating a property management business. Obviously, managers should seek appropriate legal counsel to ensure their own compliance in their locale.

While some will not be applicable to particular management firms, in general these laws include the following:

1. **Environmental laws** outline the limits of air, water and/or noise pollution.
2. **Energy conservation laws** are usually enacted at the local level and enforced through local utilities, although they may be written into building and other codes.
3. **Landlord/tenant laws,** usually in the form of statutes and ordinances, are basic to the operation of all rental property. They deal with such issues as leases, evictions, forcible detainers and abandonment.
4. **Tax laws,** in general, are the most variable of the local laws with which you should be familiar, not only for tax purposes, but also for tax protest or appeals procedures on behalf of your clients.
5. **Fair housing laws** generally deal with discrimination, subsidies and certain aspects of home construction.
6. **Rent control laws** attempt to mandate "affordable housing" by restricting rent increases.
7. **Land use laws** deal with such restrictions as zoning, densities and setbacks.
8. **Health and safety laws,** despite the federal Occupational Safety and Health Administration (OSHA), remain primarily a local function. They include laws regarding fire prevention, electrical usage, restroom cleanliness, refuse disposal, security, sewer/septic tank uses, etc. Government agencies have considerable authority in this area and managers must know the inspection procedures.
9. **Employment laws** can be found on both the federal and state levels. Primary concerns involve the Federal Wage and Hour Act, the Equal Employment Opportunity Act, the Age Discrimina-

tion in Employment Act and other civil rights acts. Managers should obtain advice on these laws from local resource organizations, because they are difficult to understand and the provisions within them are constantly being reinterpreted by the courts.

10. **Government regulations** and other legal requirements that are similar from locale to locale include the need for a business license and permits, the posting of warning and/or advisory signs, limitations on gambling, stipulations on the frequency of official inspections and the requirements for and limitations on contracts and licenses.

11. **Worker's compensation laws** provide for the medical and economic care of an employee who is injured on the job. It is not always possible to avoid the situation in which an independent contractor performing a one-time service is allowed to collect against your company's insurance. Managers must nonetheless be aware of the traps in these laws.

REAL ESTATE LAWS

Specific to the operation of a property management company as a business are such legal issues as agent and contract law and various breaches, intended or otherwise, of responsibility and trust. Some of the following areas, for example, may be included in the real estate broker licensing law of your state. In many cases in which complaints are brought against a property management firm under these laws, they will be filed both in the court system as a civil suit and with the real estate licensing entity of the state government as a licensing violation.

Law of Agency

Property management firms (and managers themselves) are *agents* in that they are authorized by clients—the owners of property—to act on their behalf. As it applies to property management in general, the law of agency requires the firm (the agent) to care for, protect and exercise such judgment in the stewardship of the property as if it were the agent's own.

Contracts define the scope of this authorization as well as provisions for its termination. These contracts, while they may also be oral, should always be in writing.

Fraud

Fraud is partially defined as a willful misrepresentation intended to deprive someone of a right. It can be a crime or a tort, an offense against a person as opposed to one against the public. In some instances, fraud may be equated with a false pretense, which is a crime. Normally, a charge of fraud will be closely related to a companion breach of contract complaint.

Frauds are of two types: actual or constructive. *Actual fraud* requires that the act be motivated by a desire to deceive and, therefore, can never be the result of an accident. Actual fraud can include a lie, failure to disclose information or a statement made in reckless disregard of true fact.

Constructive fraud is the result of misconduct that arises when a profit (not necessarily financial) is made from a relationship of trust. One example of constructive fraud occurs when a property manager, in the course of selling or buying on behalf of a client, receives an undisclosed fee or other consideration (often referred to in nonlegal terms as a kick-back).

Because constructive fraud can be inferred from faulty records, it is vitally important that property managers carry out their confidential and fiduciary responsibilities with the utmost care. Employees should be told not to represent anything as true unless they know it is true; they must be encouraged to look into matters for themselves rather than take someone else's word.

Commingling

Combining funds from different sources into a single account is *commingling*. What the real estate industry and the law are particularly concerned with here is the placement of a client's funds into an agent's (i.e., property management company's) personal account.

Not only is commingling an invitation to allegations of fraud, it also can result in the client's money being attached or frozen if legal action becomes pending against the agent. As such, property managers are responsible for setting up (and using) trust fund accounts for clients and maintaining accurate records of all transactions. Your integrity is at stake here. Being found guilty of commingling will destroy your business and will likely result in the revocation of your license.

To ensure against commingling, make certain that at least two employees are involved in any money transactions. If your company is small and can't afford two money people, let one handle the company account and you, personally, handle the client's account.

Contracts

It is important that property managers review all contracts with a client before they are signed. It is not enough to have the signature on the dotted line, since a client may later disclaim the signature on grounds of undue influence (i.e., he or she took your word for it). Some property management firms even have their clients sign a separate agreement stating that they have read the contract, understand its provisions and were not under undue influence or otherwise pressured into signing it. An additional tactic in the area of tenant contract enforcement is to have signatures witnessed by another party.

Another excellent consideration is to have an information sheet filled out and signed by the tenant and/or you or your agent on behalf of your client at the time a lease contract is signed. Such a sheet should contain auto identification and tag numbers, employer's name, address and telephone number, tenants' social security numbers, dates of birth and physical descriptions (the latter will be needed by process servers or police). This information may be necessary in order to collect on a judgment. Your jurisdiction, for example, will probably allow you to subpoena a party to a postjudgment debtor's exam. But if the party fails to appear, you may be allowed to get an arrest warrant if you can provide a description and date of birth.

Negligence, Incompetence and Responsibility

Proven negligence or incompetence is cause for action of one sort or another in all states. The managing agent (i.e., the principals of the firm) have a legal duty to reasonably supervise the company's property managers. You can lose your real estate license not only for wrongful acts you or your employees commit in the state where you base your operations but also, in some cases, for acts that take place in other states.

All of these actions are likely to show up in record keeping long before they become legally obvious; this is another reason to keep scrupulous records.

Antidiscrimination

These laws, which provide for civil action by people claiming discrimination on account of race, color, religion, national origin or sex, can be found at every level of government.

This is a difficult yet vital area of concern, because there are many antidiscrimination laws, with new ones being added and new interpretations for old ones being determined all the time. As is true for all areas of responsibility, the agent (company) is accountable for alleged acts of discrimination by employees and hired subcontractors. Here again, it is advisable to have a written company policy concerning matters of discrimination and have all employees and subcontractors sign and date a statement to the effect that they have read the document and understand its provisions.

Discrimination claims are not usually made until after a significant event has taken place (such as a dismissal or lack of a raise or promotion) and that the alleged indignity, which may be totally unrelated to the triggering event, may have been going on for quite some time. Managers can best protect themselves here by being aware of the social aspects of work and cultivating an informal channel of information that will allow access to gossip, as well as having periodic private reviews with employees.

Landlord/Tenant Law

Every state has some type of landlord/tenant law. It is the basic law that governs rental properties and one of the key guides for operation within the local concepts of the law.

The purpose of this law is to protect the health, safety and investment of both tenants and owners. It sets forth standards for the physical features and operation of properties, and creates detailed regulations to carry out the law's intent.

As the field of residential rentals has become more complex, some states have created separate statutes for residential landlord/tenant law and commercial or general landlord/tenant law. A few states have even enacted a third statute pertaining specifically to mobile home parks.

In every case, this law is a highly complex piece of legislation that can be easily misunderstood or misinterpreted. Study your local version carefully. Understanding it will reduce legal and administrative problems.

SPIRIT OF THE LAW

Because laws are based on societal ethics and morality, they have a sense of spirit or intention as well as a hard definition. The courts refer to this intention as public policy. As such, laws can usually be altered if the result makes them more responsive. For example, while policies and/or standards must at least comply with the law's minimum, higher standards may be set when dealing with a special set of facts. Therefore, you must be aware of the public policy reasons behind the laws so that you can better develop the company policies and regulations that are your management responsibility.

Be aware that local agencies will inspect a property, upon request, to ensure compliance with local laws and regulations. Of course, during these inspections, they will cite violations of which you may be unaware. If you are lucky enough to be managing a property with a history of violations, inspections will occur periodically without an invitation. Take a personal interest in these inspections and reports. If the property's utilities are turned off as a result of your inattention, rest assured that your client will not be happy.

Inspections are valuable, and you should maintain a positive attitude during the process. They protect the tenant against accidents and hazardous conditions and the property owner (your client) against lawsuits and inferior work by subcontractors, all of which could lead to embarrassing management/client relations.

MANAGEMENT CONTRACTS

Most management companies will be concerned with three basic types of contracts: (1) management/owner agreements, (2) tenant/homeowner contracts and (3) contractor service/construction agreements.

Management companies must first establish an agreement with the property owner before taking on a new project. This management/owner agreement should be a written contract that covers in detail what each party expects of the other (a sample property management agreement may be found in Appendix D). In general, a management agreement

- is an employment contract;
- establishes the owner's relationship to the management company and transfers power of attorney to the manager;
- spells out the rights, responsibilities and limitations of managers and owners/clients so as to avoid misunderstandings;
- states the amount of money that will be paid for management services; and
- provides for termination of services.

Specifically, any management agreement includes

- general terms;
- signatures of all owners;
- exact commencement and termination dates;
- description of the property (including a legal description);
- authority to execute/negotiate leases/contracts (i.e., power of attorney);
- repair and maintenance duties (including the procedure for non-budgeted expenses and capital improvements);
- advertising clause (who is responsible for advertising and promotion);
- hold-harmless or indemnification clause;
- insurance responsibility for procuring, paying and delineating coverage (amount and identification of those insured on liability and errors and omissions (E&O) policies);

- bank accounts (clauses concerning commingling, trustee accounts, ownership of accounts, protection against failure of a deposit, etc.);
- conditions for termination for causes other than normal (see Chapter 5);
- employees to be managed;
- exclusive right to lease and to list the property for sale if the owner decides to sell;
- fees and manner of payment;
- accounting and report generation (type, frequency, etc.);
- management plan (if required);
- collection of rents and other income; and
- payment of taxes and mortgages.

Within the above context, most property management company contracts usually have provisions to

- review annually all insurance coverage to determine whether it is adequate and economical;
- require valid copies of worker's compensation and liability coverage for all contractors before engaging in work for the property;
- supply a 24-hour emergency phone service (if required);
- arrange for an annual audit (uncertified) and preparation of federal and state returns by an outside accounting firm;
- handle all payroll and file all quarterly reports (work with the accountant, and prepare all forms, reports and returns required by the law as it relates to the employees);
- obtain contracts for all utilities, extermination and lawn service, major pool repairs, painting, common area insurance and other such services as may be necessary;
- arrange for the completion of takeover and termination procedures on the properties;
- maintain businesslike relations with all owners; and
- confer with owners on important matters.

Tenant Agreements

Leases are (or should be) written occupancy agreements. Because of vagueness or interpretational concerns over various laws, current ethical practice compels that most leases generally favor the tenant. As with management agreements, they should be written to avoid misunderstandings and reliance on memory as well as to provide a basis for arbitration or, if necessary, a lawsuit.

Items that should be in a lease (depending on the type of property) include

- description of area being leased;
- parties involved (i.e., tenant, owner);
- rent (how much, when due, method of payment, escalation clause, etc.);
- term;
- security deposit;
- condition of area being leased;
- right of entry;
- rules and regulations (separately signed and dated);
- waivers of rights (may be illegal in some states);
- exculpatory clauses (responsibility of landlord for anything that occurs in the leased area—restrictions may be illegal in some states);
- death
- military (draft or reassignment);
- occupancy restrictions;
- sublease assignments;
- condemnation provisions;
- pet limitations;
- maintenance clause;
- abandonment conditions;
- fire and casualty responsibilities;
- conditions of lease transfer;
- bankruptcy, insolvency provisions; and
- special provisions (i.e., late charges, options, improvements, other waivers, etc.).

Subcontractor and Service Agreements

Often, it makes financial sense to hire an outside contracting firm to perform certain tasks, such as plumbing, electrical or carpentry repair. Here again, there should be a written contract for these services that establishes the management company/subcontractor relationship, specifies the conditions and work to be performed and states the amount of money to be paid and the method and conditions of payment.

Service contracts should include

- general terms;
- description of work to be performed;
- exact date work is to start and be completed;

- valid copies of subcontractor's worker's compensation and liability coverage or a signed document to the effect (i.e., certificate of insurance);
- fees, conditions and manner of payment; and
- signatures for management company and subcontractor.

LIABILITY AND INSURANCE

The increased need for insurance is an unfortunate legacy of our times. The more credentials, expertise and success you have, the less tolerant many people will be of real or perceived shortcomings in performance. As such, the potential dollar loss that insurance protects can be overwhelming.

The three areas of insurance concern are protection for (1) the property owner, (2) the management company itself and (3) subcontractors. Deciding the areas of insurance responsibility (primarily through generalized hold-harmless clauses) is a major subject.

Property Owner

The property owner at his or her own expense, must obtain (or have the management company obtain) and keep in force adequate insurance against physical damage and liability or injury to the property or individuals. While the management company is usually held harmless in matters of negligence or misconduct on the part of the owner, there is a thin line that must not be crossed if it is to avoid becoming involved. In general, the management company must

- execute its responsibilities so as not to be subject to claims of contributory negligence;
- promptly notify the owner and insurance company of any loss, injury or damage;
- cooperate with the owner and insurance company in defense of any claims; and
- take no action that might prejudice the owner's defense of a claim.

In legalese, such points are stated in a management agreement as:

Manager shall furnish whatever information is requested by owner for the purpose of establishing the placement of insurance coverages and shall aid and cooperate in every reasonable way with respect to such insurance and any loss thereunder. Owner shall include in its hazard policy covering the property, personal property, fixtures and equipment located thereon, and manager shall include in any fire policies for its furniture, furnishings or fixtures situated at each property, appropriate clauses pursuant to which the respective insurance carriers shall waive all rights of subrogation with respect to losses payable under such policies.

Management Company

Management companies will usually maintain seven types of insurance coverage, which will be discussed later in this chapter. However, turnabout is fair play, and it is necessary to hold the property owners harmless in matters of negligence or misconduct on the part of the management company.

Again, in a contract, such a clause would specify that the management company shall:

> ...indemnify, defend and hold owner harmless from and against any and all claims, demands, causes of action, losses, damages, fines, penalties, liabilities, costs and expenses, including attorneys' fees and court costs, sustained or incurred by or asserted against owner by reason of or arising out of manager's and its employees' breach of this agreement, activities of which constitute intentional torts or gross negligence or intentional misconduct with respect to the duties and obligations required by this agreement to be performed by it. The provisions of this clause shall survive the expiration or termination of this agreement. It is the intention of the parties that this indemnity merely requires establishing liability by a court of competent jurisdiction or by settlement agreed to by manager and owner and does not require payment as a condition precedent to recovery by owner against manager under his indemnity.

Be aware that insurance, in the form of an errors and omissions policy, is available to provide for damages incurred due to negligence or misconduct (unintentional or otherwise). This is covered in more detail later in this chapter.

Subcontractors

To avoid potential lawsuits upon the owner and/or the management company, it must be required that all outside contractors working on the property have worker's compensation and comprehensive liability insurance in force. It should be up to the owners of the property to waive this requirement for an individual subcontractor.

RISK MANAGEMENT

A thorough understanding of the role of insurance starts with the concept of risk management, a process that essentially involves five steps to protect the asset.

1. Identify areas of potential loss.
2. Analyze the potential severity and frequency of the loss.
3. Develop alternative methods of combating the loss (avoidance, loss control, non-insurance transfer insurance).
4. Implement the best method.
5. Monitor the results.

According to this scenario, the actual purchase of insurance should be the last of your alternatives in risk management. Why? Because risk management decisions should always be based on the greatest cost/benefit relationship and insurance will always be the most expensive option in this regard.

Property managers should give serious considerations to the other options of *avoidance, loss control* or *non-insurance transfer* before purchasing insurance. It is still true that the best method for handling loss exposure is not to have any. While it may sound simplistic, the careful evaluation of potential loss can often lead to its elimination. If there appears to be no way to avoid a potential loss, the next step is to develop methods for keeping it to a minimum through loss control. Finally, non-insurance transfer, sometimes referred to as subcontractor's insurance, means that the responsibility for any potential loss is transferred to a third party.

Insurance Coverage

There are seven areas for which insurance is commonly purchased to protect the management company and (coincidentally) client/owner assets.

Property Insurance. This covers items such as buildings and their contents, equipment used in the normal course of business and the loss of business income. It may also cover such secondary or miscellaneous property as pools, fences, walls and lights.

When purchasing property insurance, keep in the mind the following general definitions:

Buildings refers to any permanent, occupied structures and includes any attached walls and/or fixtures.

Contents refers to nonpermanent property that is either within the building or within 100 feet of it and includes furniture, supplies, inventory and tools. It may also include the property of others (i.e., employees or tenants) held in your custody or care.

Business income insurance provides protection against the loss of income due to any covered damage to the building. For example, if one of your shopping centers had a fire, business income insurance would replace any lost rental income that might result from its closure.

Secondary or miscellaneous insurance will be necessary to cover property that is normally located more than 100 feet from a building; it includes such items as signs, lamps, walls, fences and antennas (e.g., satellite dishes), as well as underground electrical or plumbing hook-ups.

There are two generally recognized means of calculating the value of property for insurance purposes. *Actual cost* determines the cost of the damaged property minus depreciation. *Replacement cost* is the actual cost of replacing the item as if it were new (i.e., without regard for depreciation).

While replacement cost coverage will be prudent to consider in most cases, insurance companies will not generally insure property for actual full replacement (retail) cost. As a rule, you will be required to carry insurance for 80–90 percent of the replacement cost of the property, and you will be liable for the remainder. In effect, you will be self-insuring (or coinsuring) a part of the value of the property in question.

In most cases, this presents few problems, because most insurance companies can make arrangements to replace the damaged property within the percentage insured for. But coinsuring for much less than 80 percent, while it can be a cost-saver on paper, can be disastrous if real trouble occurs.

For example, let's say that our company is located in a building with a replacement cost of $100,000. Your insurance company says it will insure the building for replacement cost at 90 percent of its value, but you decide to insure it for only $50,000 or 50 percent. Then a fire guts your offices to the tune of $10,000.

The result: the insurance company is legally responsible for only 5/9 of the loss or $5,555. The remaining $4,445 will be your responsibility.

Coinsurance is, in effect, a form of deductible and, to a degree, it makes practical sense to reduce insurance rates if you can realistically absorb a larger than normal deductible. The cost-effectiveness of such a decision should be uppermost in your mind. Evaluate the possible severity and frequency of loss.

In most states, there are three basic levels of insurance. In order of cost-effectiveness, the causes of loss are called *basic, broad* and *special.*

Basic coverage includes fire, lightning, explosion, windstorm or hail, smoke, aircraft or vehicles, riot or civil disturbance, vandalism, sprinkler leakage, sinkhole and collapse, and volcanic action. Depending on where you are located, exclusions will apply.

Broad coverage adds to basic by including falling objects, ice, snow or sleet, glass breakage and water (but not flood) damage. Special coverage adds losses due to theft, but may exclude such theft in connection with floods and earthquakes.

Special situations or property requirements will result in special endorsements to your policy. Typical property or situations here include boilers and air conditioning units, computers, glass (especially as part of security systems), building ordinance upgrades (for bringing old buildings that have been damaged up to current code) and flood and earthquake damage.

Another form of special coverage is leasehold improvement, which covers any increase in rent for the remainder of your tenant's lease should a move to a new location be required as a result of fire and/or major destruction.

Liability Insurance.   The very nature of property management exposes a company to all sorts of liabilities, particularly if negligence can be demonstrated. Liability insurance, which does not pertain to automobiles, covers damage to property and bodily (not personal) injury to third parties. Personal injuries include libel, slander, etc., protection for which can be added under an endorsement (see above).

Liability insurance is generally available in amounts of from $300,000 to $1 million per occurrence, but larger amounts can also be purchased. The cost of this insurance, which varies according to type of possible exposure, is usually based on square footage.

Automobile Insurance.   Auto policies generally provide coverage for bodily injury and property damage due to automobile accidents. As is true of all insurance, premiums for company-owned cars can be kept low if you can absorb a higher deductible on comprehensive and collision. Some other considerations:

- It may not be cost-effective to cover older company vehicles for physical damage.
- A good preventive maintenance program will reduce situations that lead to accidents.
- Consider non-owned auto coverage if your employees use their personal cars to conduct company business.

Crime.   Television melodrama to the contrary, most crime falls into the category of losses involving property such as money or other negotiable instrument (i.e., stocks, etc.) or equipment. At least two separate policies will be necessary, because insurance companies distinguish between crimes by employees, partners or owners and those caused by outsiders. This insurance is particularly advisable when an employee normally handles large amounts of money (especially cash) or inventory or otherwise controls the checkbook.

Worker's Compensation.   Worker's compensation laws vary from state to state, but they are all mandatory for anyone with employees and they all cover work-related accidents, injuries or diseases. The insurance covers medical expenses, lost wages, rehabilitation and certain amounts of debt. Rates are based on payroll and are subject to audit by the state.

Errors and Omissions.   As the professional provider of a service, you are subject to many of the same standards as doctors, lawyers and accountants, especially because a lack of performance or error of judgment can cause a loss to a client. Regular liability insurance does not generally cover claims of this type, but errors and omissions coverage will protect you from financial trouble in the event of bodily injury, property damage or a book-keeping error.

Employee Benefits.   If your company is large enough, insurance policies for life, health and pension or profit-sharing will make sense. On the other side of the coin, a buy-sell agreement for very small companies—commonly funded through life insurance—can be a significant benefit if one or more of the principals dies. Not only does this agreement eliminate the infighting among the survivors that can often destroy a company, it also can provide employees with the names of ascension to company ownership.

Health insurance, depending on the size of your company, can be written on an individual or group basis. While it is not your concern to monitor the private behavior of your employees, it is your concern (both ethically and financially) to provide for a healthy employment environment and, through company policies and programs, encourage a healthy outlook. Studies suggest that containing health care costs through such measures as health maintenance organizations may have reached its maximum potential and that any further significant reductions in health insurance costs may be achievable only through changes in lifestyles.

An actuarial study conducted for Control Data Corporation, for example, indicated that (1) employees who smoke more than a pack of cigarettes a day had health care costs 18 percent higher than nonsmokers, (2) overweight employees generated 48 percent more claims over $5,000 than thinner employees, (3) employees with high cholesterol levels had 24 percent more claims over $5,000 than those with low levels and (4) people who did not wear auto seat belts had 13 percent higher health care costs, spending 54 percent more time in the hospital, than those who buckled up.

A wide array of health care options is available. Current standard practice is for the employer to pay for all (or a significant portion) of the employee premium, with the employee paying a small additional premium for family members, if desired. All employees must be offered identical coverage. This stipulation does not preclude employees selecting different coverages from a menu of choices (if your company policy provides such a menu), just that the menu must be identical.

The traditional method for buying health insurance is through an indemnity plan. Normally, the insured must satisfy a deductible of $100 to $250 per year; then the plan pays 80 percent of covered expenses up to $5,000 and 100 percent beyond that up to a specified amount, usually $1 million.

Pensions and profit sharing plans are generally set so that either the company contributes exclusively or the company and employee both contribute. *Contribution pension plans,* which are tax deductible, are funded by the company and are based on a fixed percentage of an employee's annual salary subject to certain limitations.

Benefit pension plans are also tax deductible and also funded by the company. The premiums paid vary for each employee, however, as they are calculated upon a predetermined retirement income and are based, therefore, on the age of the employee. Contributions are deposited into a trust fund account.

So-called *executive split dollar plans* provide for the sharing of benefits and costs by both the company and the employee. The company, however, is the subowner of the policy and the beneficiary of the employee's predetermined death benefits. The plan is not tax deductible.

Selecting an Insurance Company and Agent

While the cost of an insurance policy is of major importance, it is also important not to overlook the financial stability of the insurance company and the expertise of the agent you will be working with. It will be highly beneficial to deal through a company and agent that are familiar with the property management business.

In any event, insist on annual reviews and always notify your agent of any new potential exposures or reductions to risk. Keep a record of what insurance has been placed on the company and its properties by using an insurance summary form (see Figure 2.1).

Handling Insurance Problems

The claims of advertisements and commercials notwithstanding, there is no such thing as an easy insurance problem. In matters of client property

Figure 2.1 Insurance Coverage Summary

Property: _____   Date: _____   *Prepared By:* _____

Coverage	By (Company)	Agent and Phone #	Amt. of Coverage	Period Cvrg From	To	Annual Premium	Deduc- tible	Coins.	Comments
Property									
Liability									
Auto									
Crime									
Machinery and Boiler									
Worker's Comp.									
Errors and Omissions									
Health									
Life									
Pensions									

Instructions:
• This report is prepared annually for each property and management company.
• Other considerations on obtaining insurance are the following: plate glass, signs, flood, business interruption and vandalism.
• Some policies may combine coverage.

protection, your reputation and, therefore, your professionalism are on the line. Depending on circumstances, the situation can even degenerate into charges of negligence if the problem is not corrected quickly, efficiently and with a properly composed demeanor. The four most common insurance-related problems are described below.

Property Damage.   The insurance agent must be called immediately. It is the agent's responsibility to then alert an adjuster and authorize a contractor for repairs.

In matters such as fire damage, seal or secure the area as quickly as possible, with either fencing or a security guard, to prevent injuries to passersby and to discourage looting.

If it is safe for you to enter, you should conduct a visual review of the damage and note the equipment, personal or other content losses in writing. It is the contractor's job to determine structural damages and estimate the cost to physically rebuild. This rebuilding should include any upgrading needed to satisfy new codes and should be accomplished as quickly as possible.

If the damage is extensive enough, work with any tenants to arrange for temporary moving and leasing alternatives until the damage is repaired. Remember, you want the tenants to move back.

Liability Claims.   Record the time and date of the damage and try to establish the apparent cause of the problem. Notify your insurance company as soon as you can thereafter and obtain the police report. Use claim forms provided by the insurance company. (Note: While the insurance company will obtain a copy of the police report, you should have one for your own files.)

Take photographs of the damage and then obtain repair estimates. If it is necessary to make repairs before the insurance company acts, keep a written list of the costs and copies of all invoices.

Lawsuits and Other Legal Complaints.   Write down the date, the method of delivery and the approximate time that the lawsuit or complaint was served or otherwise received. Send a copy to the insurance company immediately.

Missing Money or Other Crime.   Notify the police immediately. Note the name of the officers who come to investigate (it may be necessary to contact or refer to them later) and be sure to request a copy of their report. If the matter is one of money, conduct a thorough audit within 24 hours.

Other Concerns

Be sure that vendors and contractors are licensed and bonded and can provide certificates of insurance, including those for general liability, auto liability and worker's compensation.

Property owner/clients should be made aware that the management company purchases insurance to protect itself from its own negligence and that the company reports such incidents to its own insurance company, which then addresses the matter. This is different from general property damage, which is reported to the client's insurance carrier.

Last, but not least, it is advisable to determine how your insurance company handles situations involving business-sponsored activities that include alcohol and establish a company policy accordingly. The liability for alcohol-related accidents and injuries can be significant. Companies have been held liable for allowing intoxicated employees to drive home after alcohol-related business activities as well as for sending employees home after they reported for work while under the influence.

3: Starting the Management Firm

Some people find themselves running property management firms through circumstances rather than conscious effort. While this can work out fine, it more often leads to tremendous problems.

Therefore, before you attempt to start a management firm, you should be able to answer four questions:

1. *What do I have to sell (i.e., what are my credentials to manage properties and can I offer something unique or at least better)?*

2. *What is my most current experience?*

3. *Who are my potential clients?*

4. *Do I really want to do this and why?*

The first three questions are ones of qualifications. The fourth is one of motive. The inability to honestly answer "yes" to the last question is a major reason for business failures in this industry. In many areas of the country, competition among qualified businesses is keen, and what separates the winners from the losers is the answer to the last question.

In 1990, for example, over 29,000 property management companies were operating in the United States, a number that represents an annual growth rate of about 17.5 percent since 1986. If we assume that this rate of growth could continue, there would be more than 175,000 property management firms by the year 2000. Even a highly conservative (but probably more realistic) annual growth rate assumption of 3 percent indicates more than 9,000 additional companies over the next 10 years (see Figure 3.1).

To prosper under these conditions takes more than ability and experience; it takes a personal motivation and dedication that will see you through the bad times as well as the good.

Figure 3.1   Growth of Property Management Firms 1986-2000 (est.)

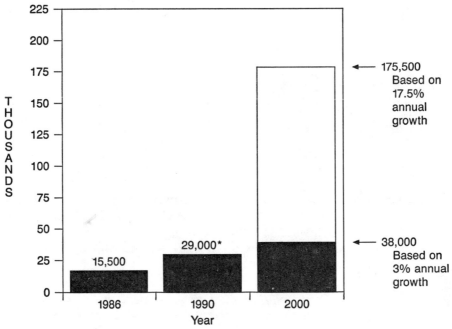

*American Business Information

This having been noted, ability and experience, particularly your most recent experience, obviously count for something. You must, however, be realistic. Years of experience with a government agency, an accounting firm, or other property management companies are a plus. But don't expect to be able to establish a property management firm for office buildings when most of your experience is in apartments.

Also, in starting a business, you will have to be aware not merely of where the marketplace is today, but also of where it is heading and how fast it is getting there. Understanding this will allow you, through organization, to control, act upon or at least see opportunities in information and events.

Chapter 1 presented a starting point. But it is not possible to determine every factor that affects the value of the industry in each market of the country. Such local matters as political climate, rent control, occupancy levels, money supply, employment and population trends can have a profound effect on the profitability of a business.

Also, whether you are starting a new property management business or buying an existing one, it is important to come to terms with your own needs. This goes beyond such jargon as long-term, short-term, present yield, security, etc. To be sure, these considerations all affect feasibility, but the success of your venture really depends on your ability to invest in people, that is, your ability to understand their idiosyncrasies and manage them to the advantage of the business.

DEVELOPING A PLAN

Although many businesspeople loathe the idea of assembling a formal business plan, a firm that does not have one wanders and is at the mercy of the marketplace. As such, a good business plan is an essential guide to success. Note the use of the word *guide*. Most business plans, for a variety of good reasons, are never actually implemented in exactly the way described. Nevertheless, they do allow you to get your thoughts on paper in a logical manner that either covers all the major considerations or points out the loopholes. Developing a business plan is also a necessary step in securing financing.

A formal, written business plan based on well-calculated goals will strengthen the resolve of owners and managers, allow for efficient action and the ability to learn from mistakes as well as successes and help keep the company ahead of the risks of change.

The Elements of the Business Plan

An outline of a basic business plan for a property management company, in question and statement form, is in Appendix C. Basically, such a plan describes the company and its industry, the specific market and the company's marketing approach, who is working in the company, how much money is needed and what the money can do for the business.

The plan should be divided into sections, as follows:

- Company description
- Management/Ownership
- Marketing plan
- Operation
- Financial plan
- Schedules

Determining Need

The research you undertake to determine whether a new property management company is needed is the basis for the business plan and can help you make the right decisions. However, don't rely solely on research as the basis for your decisions; use your own perceptions as well.

This is not to say that research should always support perception (we would not need research if this were so), but that the best research explains what is happening and why. As such, it can be used to impress upon others the necessity for starting a new business, purchasing an existing one or refinancing an existing loan.

Under no circumstances should you start, buy or refinance a business simply because money is available. Projects that are solely money-driven are, more often than not, doomed to failure.

A preliminary analysis or forecast of demand for property management services, sometimes called a needs study, should be made in order to determine the feasibility of starting a new company. This study should provide the information necessary to establish territories based upon the number of potential customers, geographic distribution, purchasing power and other such characteristics. From here, it should be possible to target potential clients or establish quotas (i.e., the major goal or objective) based on the number of properties, the dollar volume of potential fees or even the number of calls made to potential clients.

Figure 3.2 presents guidelines for a needs study, which should help you answer the questions that follow.

Figure 3.2   Outline for a Needs Study

1. **Determine the general market for real estate with respect to**
   A. General growth/antigrowth trends
   B. Seasonal trends
   C. Size and type of uses

2. **Evaluate the competition by**
   A. Location
   B. Type of property specialty
   C. Size

3. **Review the proposed location for the business in light of**
   A. Attractions/advantages
   B. Disadvantages
   C. Status of nearest competition

4. **Develop cost factors**
   A. Office rent costs
   B. Projected operating costs (including financing)

5. **Calculate pro forma financial statements based on**
   A. Costs
   B. Projected market capture

6. **Develop conclusions about**
   A. Marketing feasibility
   B. Financial feasibility

1. *Is there a market for a property management company in the area?*

2. *What kinds of people live or work in the area (e.g., a large retirement market, young professionals, lawyers, bankers)?*

3. *How many and what kinds of people are moving into the area?*

4. *What type of development appears to be the most successful?*

5. *What are the present vacancy and absorption rates?*

6. *Is zoning selective?*

7. *Are utilities readily available at reasonable rates?*

8. *What is the tax situation?*

9. *Are there any unusual or prohibitive health or other special restrictions?*

10. *Is public transportation available?*

11. *What would be the benefits to you and the community of having a new business in the area?*

Methods for Needs Study. According to an old saying, good judgment comes from experience while experience comes from bad judgment. Although all of us eventually find "truths" to guide us in business as well as in life, bad judgment is likely to arise from relying too much on past experience as a guide to the future. This is because specific situations and events rarely present themselves twice, and it is difficult to rely solely on past success and failure in light of this change.

Another possible method is experimentation. In this course of action, each possible answer is tried out to see what happens. Experimentation is effective in many areas of business decision making, such as the development of prototypes or small-scale product development and market testing. In this respect, starting a new business on a part-time basis can be considered a form of experimentation.

Nonetheless, it is very expensive, and the decision to start your own business should not be based on an experiment.

It is difficult to find an effective substitute for research and analysis, particularly when measurable, quantitative techniques can be applied. Such operations research can include statistical analysis and the use of computer programs to simulate several different marketing or income (fee) approaches.

Of course, while your decision should not be made on the basis of research alone, such data can confirm what you already intuitively feel. In any event, research data will be invaluable in impressing prospective clients and certainly local finance and government officials.

Based on the results of your study, it should be possible to establish the general location for your business and conduct a more in-depth census. Of course, there is no magic formula for determining where to establish a new business. Statistics and perception are equally important, as is determining what effect, if any, growth in the area may have on the future.

Also, in order to evaluate whether an area will be able to support a new property management business, it may be necessary to consider developing a niche. Try to find a specialized type of property management based on a needed service that is not now being offered by other companies.

U.S. Census Bureau data can be most helpful here. The U.S. Government Printing Office offers an annual *Census Catalog and Guide*, and you can also obtain a free telephone listing of bureau subject specialists. Specialized bureau reports can target almost any geographic or political boundary down to the ZIP code or even neighborhood level.

Determining the potential number of clients can be based on the following:

- Calculate the current number of properties that, in your opinion, should be making use of property management services. Much of this information is available from the Census Bureau and local research materials from banks, government agencies, business newspapers and magazines or trade associations. Note these on a map and separate by ZIP code.
- Note the number of existing management companies and the approximate amount of business (number of clients) they have. You can begin to determine this from a good local *Yellow Pages* directory. Add to this information the size of each company (again, local government agencies and trade associations are a good source) to determine the amount of business each can reasonably be expected to handle. Note each company on a map and by ZIP code. This will help cluster the competition.
- Note general growth (or antigrowth) patterns and seasonal trends. Remember that markets are created in areas adjacent to those with an antigrowth sentiment or a moratorium on development. In terms of seasonality, mobile home parks, for example, are a seasonal management operation in many parts of the country. Again, this information is readily available from a number of local sources including Chambers of Commerce.
- The number of potential clients available to you is essentially the total number of properties that can use property management services minus those already being serviced.

The next step is to get some idea of what kind of business you can reasonably expect. First analyze the characteristics of the properties not being owner-managed. What types of properties are they? What services do they need and why aren't they getting them (e.g., cost, location)?

Once you have answered these questions, it should be possible to determine a maximum/minimum client base. That is, (1) what percentage of clients now being served might move to your new company and (2) what percentage of potential clients not now being served will become actual clients?

Although the use of statistics is important in these calculations, it's possible to make mistakes. Chief among them is the desire to extrapolate information. Information gathered last year is not necessarily pertinent today. Plans for every potential new business should be based on facts that are as current as possible.

Sources of Information. Several simple checks will help you determine the overall health of the property management market in almost any community.

First, valuable information can be obtained from the Chamber of Commerce, including population trends as well as community, commercial, residential and industrial growth patterns.

Another good source of information is the local property management association. It is to the advantage of all that good property management businesses be developed and maintained in any particular area. If, for example, a local association tells you that its members have been losing business to out-of-state companies, it might be due to a shortage of acceptable local firms. If so, the association will give you every encouragement. On the other hand, if membership in the association is low, it might be because demand is low.

The owners and managers of existing property management companies can also furnish reliable information and valuable insights. There are two things to remember here: (1) any business is a reflection of the people who run it; and (2) good property management company operators encourage healthy competition. Having lunch or otherwise meeting with the operators of existing property management firms will give you an opportunity to analyze the local competition in terms of quality as well as quantity. Through such meetings, you should be able to determine whether there is (1) an oversupply of substandard property management businesses that might suggest demand for a superior one or (2) a need that is not being met by present firms.

Property owners, your potential clients, are an invaluable source of information and will generally talk about what they need, as well as what they're not getting.

Last, be sure to visit the local planning department. Records here are public property, and it should be relatively simple to discover pending development plans, new zoning areas and restrictions.

UNDERSTANDING A BUSINESS ORGANIZATION

Few people actually start a business thinking about how it will be organized. That's because organization is a function of need; jobs are created because there is work to be done. To be sure, it is not unheard of for work to be created in order to retain an employee who is perceived as particularly valuable. Although that may serve a particular business strategy in the short term, it is rarely advantageous over the long term and usually leads to a dissatisfying relationship (see also Chapter 5). Especially for a new business, all employees must be working at peak efficiency at jobs that have real meaning to the health and prosperity of the company.

Nevertheless, thinking about organization is a necessary and valuable exercise.

The Legal Structure

Basic to the structure of a company (and its ability to secure funding) is the legal form in which it will be organized. Although the specifics are best discussed with a lawyer, the three most common business forms are:

Sole Proprietorship.   It is difficult to surpass the speed of decision making in a sole proprietorship: only one person makes all the decisions. On the other hand, capital acquisition can be limited by this arrangement, and it is difficult for one person to know everything.

Partnership.   Multiownership solves the knowledge crunch, but unless duties are very specifically outlined to everyone's satisfaction, management can be difficult. Also, although partnerships can help alleviate capital acquisition problems, limited partners have no obligation beyond their actual contributions. In this situation, outside capital may be difficult to obtain.

Corporation.   In a corporation, any liability incurred by employees is limited. Both public and private corporations can raise capital by selling stock, which is freely transferable.

One disadvantage of a corporate structure is that management decisions are essentially accomplished by committee. Also, because the corpora-

Figure 3.3   A Typical Organizational Pyramid

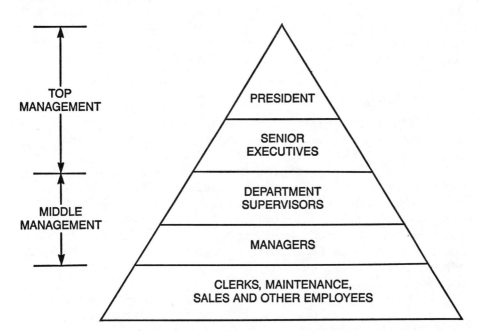

tion is a separate legal entity, its profits are subject to tax, and stockholders are taxed again.

While number of stockholders in a company may vary, majority stockholders' interests are protected through their ability to participate directly in the management process. Minority stockholders, on the other hand, are usually in a much less favorable position in this regard. However, because (1) stockholders can help promote the company, (2) they may be employees of the company and (3) it is required by law, management should actively pursue a policy of directing the company in the best interests of all.

Hierarchy

In most organizations, levels of authority are arranged in a hierarchy depending on the type of work being performed. This immediately results in two or more levels of authority and creates superior/subordinate relationships for every position in the structure.

Although the number of levels varies greatly from company to company, the structure is typically represented as a pyramid (see Figure 3.3). This arrangement is the result of an inverse relationship between the number of people involved and the kind of work being performed. The large base of the structure indicates that the number of individuals working at this level tends to be large. The structure tapers upward because at each succeeding level the need for people decreases as the need for leadership, planning, control and other managerial activities increases.

Employee Management and Structure

Although management of employees, per se, is covered more completely in Chapter 5, it is important to discuss certain management techniques that will affect the structure of the company.

At the middle level, effective management is directly related to the number of employees being managed. According to one school of thought, three to eight people is a good range. Still, mathematics tells us that any eight numbers can be arranged in several thousand combinations. Managers, therefore, turn over various aspects of their responsibilities to subordinates in order to manage relatively large groups. This practice is usually referred to as the delegation of authority or responsibility, but it can also be considered the decentralization of duties.

In stark contrast, top management is almost always concerned with the operation of the company as a whole and operates on the basis of centralized authority. Here, it should be pointed out that the top managements of major corporations are reconsidering the concept of centralization after examining the effectiveness of many foreign companies with structures that appear to be less rigid.

The actual amount of decentralization in a company varies, but it is greatest when many and/or important decisions are made by lower level managers or when the organization wishes to encourage companywide participation in decision making. Decentralization is almost always necessary, for example, in businesses with a wide variety of services and locations, or when they increase (or decrease) in size.

Leadership, the process by which an individual directs, guides or otherwise influences the work of others, is closely related to how authority is passed down through an organization. There are two basic types of leaders: authoritarian and democratic. Authoritarian leadership occurs when decision-making powers rest with one individual. The authoritarian leader assigns tasks, provides facilities and gives direction without consulting those who carry out the assignment. Decisions can be made quickly by an authoritarian leader. However, subordinates whose opinions or recommendations are not sought often feel frustrated.

Democratic leadership is best illustrated by the committee approach, in which the leader attempts to guide the group toward an objective. Democratic leadership implies participation and utilization of opinion.

Figure 3.4   Initial Organizational Chart

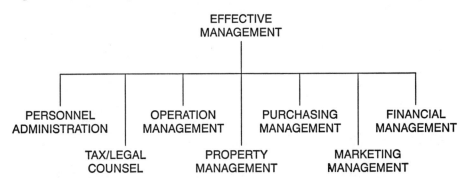

Organizational Structures

Many tasks must be completed in a typical property management firm. The various areas of managerial responsibility are illustrated in Figure 3.4.

This chart is useful only for illustrating areas of responsibility and is not to be confused with an actual working corporate structure. Property management organizational structures are normally classified into three types: line, line-and-staff and function.

Line Organization.   The typical line structure, also referred to as the military structure, is the oldest form of organization in existence. It consists of established, direct, vertical relationships that connect the positions of each level of responsibility with those above or below it. Authority extends in a direct line from superior to subordinate. The following is a simple example of this type of corporate structure.

This type of organization has two outstanding characteristics.

- Each individual reports to only one superior.
- Departments or levels are not supported by any type of overall corporate service groups.

With respect to the second point above, note that there is no accounting or marketing department visible in the structure. These services or functions are overseen by each individual manager or by a general manager and are, therefore, considered internal to each department or level.

Because of its obvious simplicity, this type of organization is normally limited to small property management firms. Still, the general concept—which provides for definite upward and downward communications—is an indispensable part of all organized effort.

Figure 3.5   Line Organizational Structure

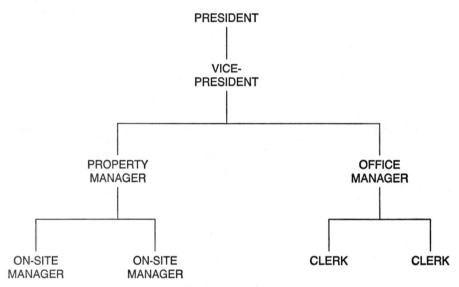

Line-and-Staff Organization.   In a line-and-staff organization, staff or advisory service departments are created to aid the line organization. These departments provide specialized assistance and, as such, are not independent. They perform their functions at the request of the rest of the line organization.

For example, in most organizations, accounting is a staff department performing accounting management functions for each of the line divisions as well as for the company as a whole. The following diagram illustrates an organization chart of a line-and-staff structure.

Advantages of the line-and-staff organization are the following:

- Technical problems are addressed by specialists or experts working with line personnel.
- Line authority is retained but flexibility in the organization is improved by means of the staff specialists who may cross departmental lines.

The disadvantages of this structure normally stem from relationships established between line-and-staff personnel, in that staff positions have no authority. Therefore:

Figure 3.6   Line-and-Staff Organizational Structure

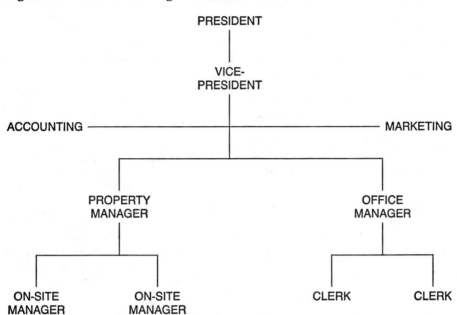

- Staff members sometimes attempt to assume administrative control over line functions.
- With no direct authority over line personnel, the staff specialist's advice may not be considered or implemented.
- Conversely, staff specialists may fail to consider line personnel in the development of plans.
- Decisions may be slowed by line personnel who tend to rely upon staff advice and recommendations before taking any actions.

Functional Organization.   Here, we begin to make full use of the principle of specialization first found in the line-and-staff organization. But while staff personnel are assumed to serve in an advisory capacity in the line-and-staff structure, in the functional structure they are in positions of authority.

The functional organization, in essence, applies the principle of specialization to each job; each employee has authority and exercises command over his or her particular function. This type of organization is seldom found in its pure form, but is significant because of its theoretical value and major influence: the development of the concept of authority for staff specialists in line-and-staff organizations.

Figure 3.7   Functional Organizational Structure

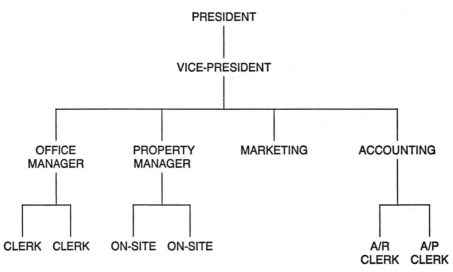

The principal advantages of the functional type of organizational structure include

- extensive use of specialists;
- planning function that is separate from manual work; and
- narrowness of responsibility permits effective selection and training of each individual employee.

Disadvantages include

- the overlapping authority that results in employees being supervised by many; and
- the generally unworkable nature of the arrangement on a corporate-wide basis, as supervisors exercising equal authority over common subordinates makes coordination difficult.

BUYING AN EXISTING PROPERTY MANAGEMENT BUSINESS

Often, it is easier to buy an existing property management business than to start a new one. Information on such businesses can be found through a broker, whose package should include the following:

- Name and address of the business
- Age of the business
- Number of clients
- Operating statement
- Furniture and fixtures
- Sale price and terms
- Current market study of the area, including competitive businesses

Answering Important Questions

With this basic information at hand, you can then do your own analysis. Before examining numerical details, however, remember that the major factor affecting your decision to buy will be to confirm why the business is for sale.

To be sure, there are many legitimate reasons why a profitable business would be up for sale (e.g., retirement, illness, lost desire), but other reasons could include increased competition, neighborhood changes, new highway construction and obsolete operating facilities.

The following are some basic questions you should be asking:

1. *Is the business an individual proprietorship, a partnership or a corporation? (The answer will affect the complexity of the transaction.)*

2. *What personal property is included (e.g., furniture, equipment, inventory, etc.)?*

3. *Was a substantial investment made in the business and/or its location before the company was listed for sale?*

4. *Is the sale the result of a bankruptcy or foreclosure? Are there unpaid taxes or contracts, pending suits or other obligations not noted in the broker's package?*

5. *Is there the appearance of unwillingness to explain, or ignorance of, pertinent facts?*

Once you have acceptable answers to these questions, you can concentrate on determining the value of the business to your own satisfaction. This is a matter of judgment and personality as well as numbers, because buying and selling is a personal decision that must feel right as well as look right.

To begin the process, gather more specific information about three areas of the business: the economic base, quality, and age. Only when you are satisfied with this information should you begin to delve into the numbers.

The Economic Base

The economic base of both the business and the general area of its location is important to your ability to obtain new clients, make improvements or even meet payroll during a slow period.

Some issues to consider:

1. *Is rent control in effect, or is it likely to be in the future?*

2. *Does the business have signed vendor contracts, or is there an opportunity to establish them?*

3. *What management agreements have been established?*

4. *Have special financial arrangements been made with clients? Remember that one cannot assign property management contracts. Be careful how the contracts are written, and make sure that the client will accept the new owners of the management company.*

5. *What is the real opportunity for obtaining new clients or raising fees?*

Quality

The questions to ask about the quality of the business include:

1. *Does the business offer potential for appreciation due to improvements that can be made?*

2. *Are there problems that could lead to costly expenses sometime in the future?*

3. *What is its image in the community?*

4. *What is the image of its current and potential clients and does it fit into the type of portfolio you want to develop?*

Age

Ask questions such as the following about the company's age:

1. *Will the business require extensive upgrading of equipment?*

2. *Will you have to move it?*

3. *Will you need to hire (or fire) employees?*

Determining Feasibility

The specific information that you've now collected should lead you to the real numbers—the total feasibility—of the project. Of course, it may be impossible for you to determine accurately some of these items yourself, let alone what they might mean to the future health of your business. In this case, hire professionals. An appraiser, especially, can be an invaluable ally.

An accountant should check:

- Financial history
- Claims (past and pending)
- Receivables

A lawyer should check:

- Chain of legal title
- Mortgages, liens (if real property is involved)
- Restrictions on ownership
- Building regulations
- Labor restrictions

A marketing consultant should check:

- Basic economics
- Long- and short-range demand
- Marketing demographics
- Overall business analysis—prospects for success or failure

Once the property management business is considered to be in good shape, then other considerations are necessary. Primarily, your concern here should be whether the business can fulfill your objectives with regard to one or more of the following considerations:

- Financial safety (Don't buy a salary.)
- Periodic benefits
- Appreciation of value
- Tax benefits

Only then should you assess the validity of the asking price and make the buying decision.

THE ACTUAL BUYING DECISION

How do you determine the fair market value of the property management business you wish to purchase? Obviously, you want a fair return on your investment after paying salaries and other expenses. To determine that return, you must calculate the present and future earning power of the business. Past earning power is merely an indicator here, because your rate of return will be earned in the days and years to come. If the business will not give you a future rate of return at least equal to that for another, comparable investment, then it is probably not a good buy.

Projected Earnings

Under no circumstances should you consider buying a business (or any investment property, for that matter) unless there is a possibility that its earning power can be increased.

Study the past earnings record of the business. Go over a profit and loss (P&L) statement that covers the last five to 10 years. You should be interested not just in numbers, but also in relationships and trends, particularly as they pertain to

- gross income,
- gross income versus costs,
- the cost of labor and
- advertising and marketing costs.

Also compare the earnings of the business to those of the industry in general.

Begin your attempt to project future earnings by asking for the seller's own estimates, through a projected operating summary and a projected cash flow. Compare these estimates with statements showing the past performance of the business. If they differ, ask why.

About Goodwill

Goodwill is the value of intangibles, the difference between an established and successful business and one that has yet to establish itself and achieve success.

If the business meets your criteria, you should be amenable to paying for goodwill as long as it is based on the future earning power and potential of the business, not past investments of time and money.

The Purchase Price

Generally, there are two methods for determining an acceptable purchase price for an existing property management business: (1) market value and (2) capitalized or income value.

The market value approach is the more common but not necessarily the preferred method. It establishes value by simply comparing the business you are looking at with similar businesses that have been recently sold, adjusting for any differences.

The capitalized or income approach bases value on the flow of net operating income that is anticipated. This is the preferred method, as it forces both parties to examine trends that will affect future performance, which is what is really being sold and bought.

By definition, the capitalized or income value of a business is the monetary value of the property necessary to bring in a specified amount of earnings at a particular interest rate. The general formula is:

$$Capitalized\ Value = \frac{Net\ Operating\ Profit}{Rate\ of\ Return}$$

Here, net operating profit is the gross income minus all operating expenses. The rate of return is the current rate of return for similar investments (expressed as a decimal). For example, if the average net operating income over the next five years is $15,000 annually ($175,000 gross income minus $160,000 operating expenses), and the desired rate of return is 10 percent, then the capitalized value of the business is:

$$\frac{\$15,000}{0.10} = \$150,000$$

The final figure should be balanced by the going rate (the market value) of similar businesses in the area.

BASIC BUYING PROCEDURE

Once you are satisfied that the business is a good buy and that financing can be secured, you can begin the purchasing procedure, which is similar to that for purchasing any real estate investment:

1. The business is put up for sale.
2. An offer is made to the seller stating the price and terms: the percentage of down payment, the amount to be carried as a loan, the

interest rate of the loan and the amount of earnest money deposit.

3. If the offer is not accepted, further negotiations may take place.
4. Acceptance can include the approval of certain conditions before there is an actual contract, such as inspection of books and records, inspection of the physical property and equipment reviews and proper financing availability.
5. An escrow is established, calling for an impartial third party to complete the paperwork necessary to process the transaction. Some states require that lawyers perform these tasks; others accept commercial escrow companies.
6. The escrow company (or lawyer) checks all public records pertaining to the business to see if there are any claims against it, such as unpaid taxes, judgments or liens. The necessary documents are then prepared, which may include the agreement for sale; any deeds transferring real estate; bill of sale, including personal property; and promissory note (if necessary).

The final execution and completion of all documents, or the closing of escrow, results in legal recording of the transaction, usually at the county recorder's office. Funds are then transferred from buyer to seller and the sale is completed.

This, of course, is an overview. An attorney should always be present to oversee the entire transaction.

4: Office Administration

The principles of modern management require a high degree of organizational skill to support what is a large investment in people. And while the method, approach or technique to this organization is a function unique to each firm (and manager), it almost always encompasses planning, coordinating (or organizing), directing and controlling the work of others. Without exception, all of this takes place in an office.

OFFICE LOCATION

A crucial concern for a property management business is the matter of location. Since property management is a service business, it would seem to make optimum sense to have an office that is central to the properties being serviced. Unfortunately, this is a simplistic ideal that, in view of today's complex interests, is only one of several areas to consider. Among those areas are

- adequate transportation facilities (including travel time for employees to the office);
- sufficient parking;
- convenience to other service businesses (e.g., banking, shopping, restaurants);
- convenience to properties being managed;
- public relations and advertising value of location;
- opportunity for additional business; and
- the management company's priorities.

Certainly, other items must be considered, including how much space you really need (which is not to be confused with how much you really want) and its cost. A typical property management firm should probably spend no more than 4 to 9 percent of its annual gross income on basic office space.

The owner of a small company, therefore, might consider renting. This arrangement leaves substantial capital for other operational purposes and its flexibility allows the business to change locations as new business opportunities present themselves.

On the other hand, for a large company, owning (and managing) its own building might be a better choice. Ownership provides prestige, company identification and appreciation in value. If the building were large enough, areas not needed by the management company could also be leased to other businesses, thereby providing another source of revenue.

If company policies and plans for the future do not prohibit it, a logical location for any management company is at the site of a major property being managed. This, at the very least, eliminates convenience problems (e.g., travel expenses) for the management company.

This location strategy presents disadvantages, particularly if you plan to manage many similar (in other words, competing) properties. In this case, you will be expected to maintain a separate office, physically unassociated with any property being managed. The alternative is to give the impression of favoring one particular property, and the result will be that of putting all your eggs in one basket.

One way out of this situation, particularly if efficiency is involved, would be to establish a branch office at major property sites. This plan might be out of the question for smaller firms, but it could be a definite advantage for medium-sized to larger ones.

OFFICE AUTOMATION

So-called office automation is another area to be considered in terms of efficiency. Be aware, however, that pieces of electronic equipment, be they computers, facsimile (fax) machines or high-tech telephones, are only decision support tools. They cannot fill the gap between managerial and operations tasks.

This having been said, computers, letter-quality or laser printers, copiers and fax machines will remain important items for most office functions. Modems, which allow computers to talk to each other, are by far a more efficient method of transmitting information than fax machines, if only because transmitted data can later be manipulated without having to be re-entered into the computer. However, the issue of computer modem v. fax is a prime example of how a reasonable technology can be negated by human habit. It's simply easier (and less scary) for people to fax documents to each other. The lesson here is that, while your company should have the best tools it can reasonably afford, these tools must ultimately perform the tasks needed and wanted by the company's major investment: its people.

Managers must think through all the issues involved when purchasing electronic office equipment, if only because hardware and software capabilities change so quickly. Price, which appears to be the major determinant in most decisions in this area, is a false indicator, as it may amount to only 15 to 20 percent of the actual cost of any piece of equipment or system. Training (again, the investment in people), which few companies actually budget for, is the big item.

By far, the most important item of technology for any property management firm will be the telephone. Depending on the size of your company and the location of the properties you manage, such items as cellular phones and such services as call forwarding, voice mail boxes and even your own 800 number may be invaluable. Consider also their public relations or image enhancement capabilities, but always remember that fancy gadgets cannot take the place of old-fashioned telephone technique and courtesy.

THE HOME OFFICE

Although more than 9 million people currently work at home, recent surveys indicate that only about 13 percent actually work there full time (35 hours or more a week). Businesses best suited for such an office arrangement appear to be in the construction trades (where most employees are actually subcontractors), executive level management (part time) and independent sales, consulting or freelance work. It is little wonder that almost half the companies employing at-home workers have fewer than five employees.

Taking this into account, an *individual* independent property manager could probably run a business from home. In addition, a home office could make a feasible launching pad for a small, beginning firm.

But as a nerve center for a thriving operation, this type of office provides few advantages and many drawbacks. Chief among the drawbacks is the psychology of professionalism. Property owners expect the management companies they hire to be doing well enough (or to give the impression of doing well enough) to maintain a professional office with a professional staff. In addition, businesspeople expect to do business in an office environment and find it awkward to be in someone's home except for social occasions.

Many people view these notions as outdated but, as Samuel Clemens (Mark Twain) once put it, "The report of my death has been greatly exaggerated." In short, talk of foreign management principles, decentralized workplaces and the office of the future notwithstanding, traditional, conservative business practices will be with us for many decades to come. Thus, the owners and managers of property management companies—who are, after all, in the service business—will have to provide the type of service that their clients want and expect.

OFFICE DESIGN

Wherever the office is located, it must (1) support the basic functions of a property management business and (2) symbolize professionalism, efficiency and success to employees and clients.

In general, the office space necessary for administrative and management functions should be large enough to accommodate people, equipment and files with some semblance of comfort and order. The space should include a reception area, a common area for full staff/client meetings (which can double as a lunch room) and individual offices where people can conduct business with some privacy.

In addition, office layout can strongly influence operational efficiency. Factors to consider include the (1) flow of work, (2) flexibility of design, (3) space allocation and (4) safety and security provisions. Remember also that an attractive and comfortable work environment tends to improve productivity. Therefore, don't overlook such factors as (1) heating and air conditioning, (2) color coordination, (3) lighting, (4) use of music and (5) sound control.

Although it is not necessary to have the very latest in office decor, always remember that a poorly designed, cluttered or overly spartan atmosphere is a direct reflection, whether deserved or not, on your management capabilities.

The design of the office should also be based on function, not individual preference. While it is true that individual motivation plays a big part in the development of any company, an obvious display of personal ego will make many potential clients uncomfortable. After all, owners hire management companies on the basis of perceived (as well as real) competence. A major part of this perception is the degree to which a property owner, not a management company employee, feels important.

OFFICE MANAGEMENT

The office provides and stores the facts and information necessary for the operation of a business. Office management tasks encompass several areas.

Records, which are vital to the successful operation of any business, include accounts receivable, accounts payable, payroll and other types of transactions that may be needed by the various executives or departments of a company.

Another major part of office work is performing such computations as payroll, discounts, maintaining bank accounts, dividend payments, etc.

Filing is the orderly and systematic storage of the current and historical business records and papers of a concern so that they are available when needed.

The processing of both external and internal company communications involves letter writing, handling of telephone and other electronic communications, the recordings of proceedings and conferences and similar activities.

Records Maintenance and Management

This area of office management deals with retaining, storing, distributing and eventually destroying records. It includes such activities as the creation and use of forms, simplification of paperwork, retrieval of documents and the security of confidential records.

In the broadest sense, of course, any information that is supplied to a business relevant to its objectives can be considered a record or report. As such, this information includes not only such items as sales analyses and inventory reports, but also invoices, checks, bills and related business forms.

Creating Forms or Reports.   Keep in mind that every unnecessary document is a barrier to innovation. Forms or reports, therefore, should be kept to the minimum needed for the company to achieve its goals. Be aware, however, that two trends will always serve to carry this area of office management to extremes.

Given a particular assignment, the office staff will always seek to generate information, instructions, forms, policies and reports. Since the basic information usually comes from the people in the field (i.e., the actual property managers), this tendency adds to their workload, increasing cost.

Also, computer technology allows people to create forms and reports with such ease and speed that they are often created simply because they can be. Unfortunately, once these records are developed and enter into the corporate culture, they have a tendency to take on a life of their own.

In this regard, the so-called paperless office, supposedly wrought through computer technology, is a myth. In fact, the use of paper in any computerized office actually tends to increase, if only because of the ease with which documents can be modified and printed. It is a major management task, therefore, to keep this area under control (see the section "Forms Control," below).

Any good form or report has four key elements. First, it must be relevant, in that it contributes to the effectiveness of the company. A document that no longer serves this purpose should be discarded.

Second, the data generated must be as accurate as possible. Third, the arrangement of information must be clear, attractive, and easy to read and understand. Finally, the form must reflect the current operating status of the company.

Understand that most of the cost of forms and reports is in their use and storage, not in their development or the consumption of paper. In determining the appropriateness of forms and reports, therefore, ask the following questions:

1. *What is the purpose of this document?*

2. *What use will be made of the information?*

3. *What information will the document contain?*

4. *From where will the information originate?*

5. *Who will prepare the document?*

6. *How often will the document be prepared or used?*

7. *What period of time will be reflected?*

8. *How many copies will be needed and who will get them?*

9. *How will these copies be distributed?*

10. *What will be the ultimate cost of the document?*

Designing New Forms.   Assuming that you have determined the need for a new reporting document, your first step is to determine whether this particular "wheel" has already been invented by someone else. Since a vast number of different forms are readily available through office supply and stationery outlets, it will pay to check whether your need has already been met before you go through the trouble of designing a form yourself.

When developing a form, keep in mind that the amount of information needed should determine the size of the document, although it will pay to keep such data within standardized paper sizes for filing purposes.

Your new document must contain adequate identifying information, such as its use and purpose. The data requested should be placed in a manner corresponding to the natural flow of work. Also, remember to allow adequate space for recording the data. Other items to consider include the number of copies to be made, single- or double-side usage and the length of retention (see below). Generally speaking, document paper should be of better quality as the length of possible retention increases.

Forms Control. Forms control involves tracking all company documents as well as eliminating those that are unnecessary, repetitive or little-used, improving those that are essential and developing new ones as appropriate. This process becomes very important when the needs of a business change.

The criteria for all reports—relevancy, accuracy, clarity and currency—are the mainstay of the decision-making process here. Can any documents be eliminated without reducing the effectiveness of the company? Can any reports be combined or simplified? Is any additional information needed to make a particular document more effective? Do we really need a new form or report?

In keeping track of currently used forms, a retention schedule (see Figure 4.1) should be developed and adhered to based on:

1. The active life—how long the record must be readily available.
2. The inactive life—how long the record may be needed (for administrative, historical, research or legal purposes) but can be transferred to a less costly area of storage.
3. Government regulations—how long the record must be retained for legal, tax, regulatory or other official purposes.

Note that provisions will have to be made for retaining and storing client documents as well as those for the company. However, after a certain period of time, you can ask that the client store some records.

There is no statute of limitations concerning criminal prosecution for capital offenses, i.e., those for which the death penalty or murder is involved. As such, the cost of retention will have to be considered in light of the possibility that your records will ever be needed for this purpose.

In addition, policies will have to be established on the retention of records that bear no direct relation to any statute or law. Such records include purchase orders, occupancy and delinquency reports, budgets, surveys, inventories and logs.

Records Protection. The question of records retention is related to that of records protection, particularly from such disasters as fire, flood and theft. In all cases, the primary concern for management should be the protection of those records needed for all current operations and especially those that would be difficult to reproduce if destroyed.

Figure 4.1   A Sample Retention Guideline

3 YEARS
WAGE AND COMPENSATION

Time sheets	Payroll records
Employment contracts	Union agreements
Canceled payroll checks	Bookkeeping records

INCOME TAX

All cash receipts	Disbursements ledgers
General ledgers	Other books

5 YEARS
NONCAPITAL OFFENSES

Written contracts

7 YEARS
PUBLIC LIABILITY

Insurance policies	Letters and statements

Note: Check your own state laws on retention. Some state laws require retention of five years in civil cases and seven years in criminal cases. Contact your accountant and lawyer to be sure.

Storing duplicate records in separate areas is one possible solution. Fire-rated safes or files are another. Storing records off-site is a possibility, but the logistics involved usually makes this feasible only for records of historical use.

Remember that insurance is strictly compensation for loss, not protection (regardless of what the advertisements say). Likewise, fire and burglar alarms are protection after the fact.

Reporting Timetables.   Because reports and other such documents assist management in planning in an organized manner, they should be filled out on a timely basis and checked periodically. A basic recommended schedule of reports is outlined below.

- Monthly—delinquency and expense.
- Yearly—budgets, competitive property rent analysis and market survey.

- As needed—property inspection, tenant/occupancy profile, tenant roster, tool and equipment inventory and traffic log.

Detailed data on reporting timetables and recommended lists of forms by both function and end-user appear in Figures 4.2, 4.3 and 4.4. Most of these forms are located in Appendix E or elsewhere in this book.

Accounting Activities

Certainly, one of the main activities of office work is performing the numerical computations required for the operation of a business (payroll, bank accounts, dividend payments, etc.). Because a discussion of this area deserves greater attention to detail, the subject will be covered in Chapter 7.

Filing

Failure to purchase enough filing cabinets, folders and labels is a false economy. As noted before, despite the mythology of the paperless computerized office, most property management firms will have plenty of paper to go around, all of which will have to be stored and filed properly if it is to be of any use to management. Every company, therefore, must have an orderly and efficient filing system by which documents are properly labeled and arranged.

In matters of filing, also consider the use of a photocopying machine; you will need at least one copy of any original document that must leave the premises (the copy should be filed in the same place as the original). Also, plain-paper copies should be made of fax documents, as most fax machines use thermal paper, the text of which has a rather nasty habit of disappearing over time.

Setting Up a Filing System. A filing system must be set up in a logical order that allows for the rapid location of information. In general, each file drawer and/or cabinet must be accurately labeled and each individual file must be kept in a separate folder and properly marked. All files should be kept up-to-date, on a daily basis, if possible, and inspected quarterly to remove, store or destroy outdated records. Also, consider color-coding each of the major categories (with either colored file folders or tags) for further clarification.

The major categories that are required for an appropriate filing system are management, legal, accounting, correspondence and blank forms and reports. Do not maintain a "miscellaneous" category. This inevitably becomes a bottomless pit into which important documents disappear.

Figure 4.2   Basic Reporting Timetable for Management Reports

REPORT	As Needed	Weekly	Monthly	Quarterly	Semiannually	Annually	REPORT DUE DATE	REPORT PREPARED BY	REPORT DISTRIBUTED TO
BUDGETS					X		NOVEMBER 15th	PROPERTY MANAGER	OWNER
COMPETITIVE PROPERTY RENT ANALYSIS	X						AS REQUESTED	PROPERTY MANAGER	OWNER
DELINQUENCY			X				12th OF EACH MONTH	ACCOUNTS RECEIVABLE ON-SITE MANAGER	PROPERTY MANAGER
EXPENSE REPORTS		X	X				WEEKLY—EVERY MONDAY MONTHLY—END OF MONTH	INDIVIDUAL	SUPERVISOR
MANAGEMENT REPORT				X			15th DAY AFTER QUARTER	PROPERTY MANAGER	OWNER
MARKET SURVEY	X					X	AS NEEDED	PROPERTY MANAGER	OWNER
OCCUPANCY		X					MONDAY OF EACH WEEK	SECRETARY/ PROPERTY MANAGER	FILE
PROPERTY INSPECTION	X					X	ROUTINE—ANNUALLY	PROPERTY MANAGER	FILE
TENANT ROSTER	X						AS NEEDED	PROPERTY MANAGER ON-SITE MANAGER	FILE
TOOLS AND EQUIPMENT INVENTORY					X		SEPTEMBER 30th	ON-SITE MANAGER/ PROPERTY MANAGER	FILE
TRAFFIC LOG	X						AS NEEDED	ON-SITE MANAGER	PROPERTY MANAGER

FREQUENCY

Figure 4.3   Basic Forms List by Function

ACCOUNTING

BUDGET
CAM CHARGES SPREADSHEET
CHECK REQUEST
EXPENSE REPORT
FINANCIALS (PROFIT/LOSS, BALANCE SHEET)
PAYROLL
PETTY CASH
SECURITY DEPOSITS
TIME RECORDS
UTILITY LOG

EMPLOYEE

APPLICATION FOR EMPLOYMENT
BASIC EMPLOYEE INFORMATION SUMMARY
CHANGE OF EMPLOYMENT STATUS
EMPLOYMENT AGREEMENT
EXIT INTERVIEW
INDEPENDENT CONTRACTORS AGREEMENT
REPRIMAND

OPERATING

CHECK REQUEST
COMPETITIVE PROPERTY RENT ANALYSIS
COMPLAINT/WORK ORDER
DELINQUENCY
INSURANCE COVERAGE SUMMARY
MARKETING CHECKLIST
NEW ACCOUNT MANAGEMENT TAKEOVER AND CHECKLIST
OCCUPANCY REPORT
PROPERTY INFORMATION SHEET
PROPERTY INSPECTION
PROPERTY MAINTENANCE
RENTAL APPLICATION
SOCIAL ACTIVITIES
TENANT MOVE IN/OUT CHECKLIST
TENANT/OCCUPANCY PROFILE
TENANT ROSTER
TOOL AND EQUIPMENT INVENTORY
TRAFFIC LOG

Figure 4.3   Basic Forms List by Function (continued)

```
LEGAL
ABANDONMENT
AMENDMENTS TO RULES AND REGULATIONS
CONDITIONS, COVENANTS, AND RESTRICTIONS
CHANGE OF MANAGEMENT NOTICE
LEASES
LEASE NOTICE
LEASE SUMMARIES
MANAGEMENT AGREEMENTS
RENT INCREASE NOTICE
RENTAL TERMINATION NOTICES
RULES AND REGULATIONS
VIOLATIONS NOTICE
```

The Management File (see Figure 4.5).
- Advertising—all information and bills pertaining to advertising.
- Bids—all bids obtained from contractors.
- City/county/community information—important addresses and phone numbers (e.g., library, museum, Department of Motor Vehicles, hospitals, fire stations, city offices, etc.) plus maps, locations of shopping centers, recreation facilities, places of interest, etc.
- Furnishings inventory—a complete listing of all personal property.
- Employees—a list of all present and past employees and employee-related data.
- Insurance policies and information.
- Management reports—all completed reports to be filed here.
- Permits—permits, licenses and certificates of membership, etc.
- Utilities—for paid bills if tenants are charged for utilities on an individual basis.
- Warranties, guarantees—for all purchased or leased equipment.

The Legal File.
- Contracts—each contract to have its own folder.
- General—originals and copies of all legal documents.

The Accounting File.
- Bills—paid and due.
- Budgets—filed when completed.

Figure 4.4   Basic Forms List by End User*

ACCOUNTING

CAM CHARGE SPREADSHEET
CHECK REQUEST
EXPENSE REPORTS
PAYROLL
PETTY CASH
PURCHASE ORDER
RENT RECEIPTS
RENT BILL
SECURITY DEPOSIT
TENANT MOVE-IN/OUT
TIME RECORDS
TOOLS AND EQUIPMENT INVENTORY
UTILITY LOGS

TENANTS

CONDITIONS, COVENANTS, AND RESTRICTIONS
CHANGE OF MANAGEMENT NOTICE
DELINQUENCY
LEASES
LIEN NOTICE
RENT TERMINATION NOTICE
RENT INCREASE NOTICE
RENTAL APPLICATION
RULES AND REGULATIONS
SECURITY DEPOSIT
VIOLATIONS NOTICE

PROPERTY MANAGER

COMPETITIVE PROPERTY RENT ANALYSIS
COMPLAINT/WORK ORDER
DELINQUENCY
INSPECTIONS
INSURANCE COVERAGE SUMMARY
MARKETING CHECKLIST
NEW ACCOUNTS MANAGEMENT TAKEOVER
OCCUPANCY REPORT
PROPERTY INFORMATION SHEET
PROPERTY MAINTENANCE
SOCIAL ACTIVITIES
TENANT/OCCUPANCY PROFILE
TENANT ROSTER
TRAFFIC LOG

CLIENTS

BUDGET
FINANCIALS (PROFIT/LOSS, BALANCE SHEET)
MANAGEMENT REPORT

---

*SOME FORMS HAVE MORE THAN ONE END USER.

Figure 4.5   A Sample Filing System

Accounting	*Management*
Bills	Advertising
Budgets	Bids
Operating Statement	City/County/Area
Reports, Government	Employees
	Furnishings Inventory
Legal	Insurance
	Management Reports
Contracts	Permits
General	Utilities
	Warranties, Equipment
Correspondence	
General	
Ownership	

- Operating statements—filed when completed.
- Reports—as required by government agencies.

The Correspondence File.
- General—correspondence received from or sent to anyone other than the owner.
- Ownership—correspondence involving the owner and/or the management company.

The Forms File.   This file should contain individual folders for copies of every blank form, report, notice or document used by the office. The folders should be arranged either alphabetically or by topic.

Other Considerations.   Do not hesitate to establish other major filing categories, such as an emergency file, if it is logical for you to do so.

COMMUNICATIONS

Internal and external communications are a major part of office activity. However, remember that office matters are, by their nature, confidential. This requires standardized clerical procedures, regular office hours and limited after-hours access (that is, who is given keys).

In general, good office communications procedures demand:

- Accuracy—This applies to all correspondence and documents as well as bookkeeping and filing.
- Prompt attention—Don't let large workloads cause delays.
- Adequate supplies—Watch the inventory.
- Good files—Pay attention to filing and periodically clean out operating (not bookkeeping) files that are outdated or no longer useful.
- Courtesy and attention—This applies to visitors, tenants and phone callers.

Office Operating Manual

For effective communications, establish an administrative manual that formally and clearly establishes office practices for all employees. In general, such a manual for a property management company will require four sections:

1. **Organization.** This section—designed for all management down to first line supervisors—describes the structure of the company, its goals, job descriptions and other such matters.
2. **Policies.** Specific information on how the business operates should appear here. This section includes overall objectives and the actions that are required (see the section "Policies," below).
3. **Operations.** This contains detailed instructions on how a job is to be done. It includes accounting, legal, marketing, property and office work. (See the sample Accounting Operations Manual in Appendix B.)
4. **Information.** Orientation material designed for all employees is provided in this section of the manual. (See the sample Employee Information Manual in Appendix A.)

Two important factors must be considered in developing such manuals: (1) who will read them and (2) how they will be kept up-to-date.

Concerning the first factor, it is a good idea to write most manuals to the level of the average employee rather than that of supervisors or upper management. Write in plain English. Eliminate jargon or bureaucratic phrases, as these are designed solely to limit understanding.

With respect to the second point, keeping the manuals up-to-date, determine who will be in charge, how this person will get any changes, when changes will be incorporated and how they will be monitored for compliance.

Figure 4.6 is an outline of topics that would be covered in an office operations manual.

POLICIES

The purpose of policies is to help attain a high level of operating efficiency through one set of company standards. There is only one criterion for the development of a good policy: it anticipates and helps avoid unwanted situations. In this respect, policies provide greater flexibility than rules, as they allow for individual employee discretion.

Unfortunately, it is all too easy to confuse the meanings of such words as *policies*, *standards*, *rules*, and *procedures*, and we should spend a few moments to discuss the implications of each, especially as they affect the four areas of management: planning, coordinating (or organizing), directing and controlling the work of others.

Planning

Planning involves the most basic of the decision-making processes: what are the major goals of the company and how will they be achieved? Established goals are the objectives the company is attempting to reach and the directions for accomplishing tasks. Thus, goals are the basis for policies and standards.

The style or manner in which these policies and standards are set forth, most often referred to today as ethics, is becoming increasingly important.

Organizing

Organizing defines and orders the activities required to achieve the objectives decided on in the planning phase. *Policies*, in essence, are the basic mechanism by which employees learn how to act and interact in the most likely circumstances. not to be confused with specific rules, which are definitive, policies are statements that guide management toward making decisions.

Procedures are guidelines to the action required in a policy. They usually specify the timing and/or sequence of events. An example of how a procedure differs from a policy is as follows:

- **Policy**—The immediate supervisor will handle as many grievances as possible.

Figure 4.6   Outline for an Office Operations Manual

Administrative Procedures	Legal Procedures
• Mail/Correspondence	• State landlord/tenant laws
• Telephone coverage	• Other laws
• Filing	• Letters, forms, contracts, etc.
• Purchasing/Supplies	**Maintenance/Repair**
• Report timetable/Distribution	• "Housekeeping"
• Emergencies	**Client Relations**
• Media or government inquiries	**Marketing**
• Time off	**Insurance Coverage**
• Off-hours use of facilities	**Job Descriptions**
	Forms Control

● **Procedure**—An employee will tell his or her immediate supervisor about a grievance as well as submit the grievance in writing on a special form.

Actual *rules* are specific, definitive statements describing how something is to be done and, in this respect, differ from policies, which are generalizations. Rules require that a specified course of action be taken in a particular situation and may be reinforced by specific penalties. An example of the difference between policies and rules:

● **Policy**—All employees are to report to work on time.
● **Rule**—Three tardies will result in a loss of pay equal to the tardiness.

When establishing rules, remember that

● they must be reasonable and enforceable;
● they must be in writing, to the point and as short as possible; and
● they are not requests.

Figure 4.7   Objectives of Management

Directing

Directing involves guiding, supervising or otherwise running the organization as it operates. The objective is always to convert plans into action. This not only involves the major objectives of the company, but any more limited objectives that may be necessary to achieve them, such as improving employee skills and attitudes and the overall management of office life.

This area includes office *standards*, which are the means by which the quality or quantity or work being performed is measured. On a rudimentary basis, such factors as the number of letters typed, invoices prepared and telephone calls handled can form the basis of standards for the office.

Controlling

Control is a regulation function and, as such, should not be confused with directing. To control is to restrain activities so that they conform to plans. Controlling involves two major tasks: (1) to make certain that activities are performed in accordance with plans (policies, etc.) and (2) to evaluate results and, if necessary, take steps to correct deviations (standards).

While these four functions appear to be linear, they are, in reality, interrelated or circular (Figure 4.7). Results analyzed in the control phase, for example, might point to something amiss in planning or organization. Therefore, the ability to appreciate and implement effective change is the ultimate hallmark of vibrant management.

Good policies are important in that they not only let employees (and clients) know what to expect, but also produce consistent results. To be effective, however, they must be written down and acted upon in a consistent manner; otherwise employees not only tend to ignore them, but look upon their haphazard implementation as harassment. If a policy does not work or no longer serves a practical purpose, it should be changed or eliminated. Therefore, company policies should be reviewed annually. This is especially important in fast-growing management firms where size and goals can rapidly render policies obsolete.

To be sure, some policies may not need to be written. Employees are usually quick to pick up on these implied policies merely by observation. But be aware that *implied* is not the same as *intentional*. If policy is being determined by example, make it the right example.

The need for policies can come from many directions—management objectives, financial demands, emergencies, office needs and legal requirements, to name but a few. In 1989, for example, all recipients of federal grants or contracts for property or services in excess of $25,000 were required to certify that they provided a drug-free workplace in compliance with the Drug-Free Workplace Act of 1988.

The act required such employers to publish a policy notifying employees that the unlawful manufacture, distribution, dispensation, possession or use of a controlled substance would be prohibited. The policy had to designate the action that would be taken for violations and indicate that as a condition of employment, the employee had to abide by its terms and notify the company of any criminal drug conviction or violation occurring in the course of employment within five days. Each employee who worked on or was involved in a federal contract or grant was to be given a copy of this policy.

Among other things, this act also required the employer to establish a drug-free awareness program.

Figure 4.8 is a draft of a general company policy based on this federal requirement. While this example may be useful, please note that it is presented without regard to the unique requirements of your business.

As previously noted, all company policies are not mandated by the government, but many do get started by following certain laws or requirements that are government imposed. In this respect, labor, safety, social security and contract laws, among others, all help to shape company policy.

In an incorporated business, policies are also dictated by the articles of incorporation; company bylaws; and minutes of board of directors meetings.

The following are only a few of the policy areas that should be considered for effective operation of a property management business.

Figure 4.8 Policy on Drug-Free Workplace

AS IT IS OUR INTENT AND OBLIGATION TO PROVIDE A DRUG-FREE ENVIRONMENT, EMPLOYEES ARE EXPECTED AND REQUIRED TO REPORT TO WORK IN AN APPROPRIATE MENTAL AND PHYSICAL CONDITION. EMPLOYEES MUST ABIDE BY THIS POLICY AS A CONDITION OF EMPLOYMENT.

This company recognizes drug dependency as an illness with major health, safety and security consequences. Employees who need help in this area are encouraged to use our employee assistance program and/or health insurance plans. Efforts to seek such help will not, in any way, jeopardize any employee's job or be noted in any personnel record.

The unlawful manufacture, distribution, dispensation, possession or use of a controlled substance on company premises or while otherwise conducting company business is prohibited and violations will result in disciplinary action up to and including termination and may have legal consequences.

Employees must also report any conviction under a criminal drug statute occurring on or off company premises while conducting company business. Failure to make such a report within five (5) days of a conviction may result in disciplinary action, including termination.

This policy is mandated by the Drug-Free Workplace Act of 1988 and is in addition to other employment-related policies that prohibit use, possession, sale or working under the influence of alcohol or other controlled substances.

General Policies

- Owner's objective—The main objective of the company's owner(s) or board of directors should determine the overall policy for the business. Does the owner want to hold on to the business, maximize cash flow or sell in a short period of time?
- Financial reporting—Who will receive reports, what goes into them, how many copies and how often are they to be prepared?
- Legal—How will the company comply with all federal, state and local laws that pertain to the operation of the business? Who will be responsible for maintaining compliance?
- Change in use—The design of the company should be flexible to allow for significant business changes brought about by government action, market conditions and/or sale of the business to another party.
- Fees—The fees established should cover the costs of operating and maintaining the business in addition to providing an acceptable return on investment. The company should have a policy that reserves to it the right to calculate fees by any method desired and to change them to accommodate unexpected costs.

Office Policies

- Purchasing—How will large items be purchased? Small items? How is petty cash to be used? What about contract work?
- Recordkeeping—How will records be periodically maintained? By whom?
- Handling complaints—Who is responsible and how will complaints be noted and acted upon?
- Emergencies—What constitutes an emergency? Who should be notified (and by whom)? Where will emergency notices by posted?
- Safety—What constitutes an unsafe act? Should there be any penalties?
- Solicitations—Should solicitations of non-work-related items or services be allowed on company time? If so, under what circumstances? Should the company sponsor a charity?
- Company assets—Should company assets (e.g., office machines, equipment and supplies) be allowed to be diverted for personal use? For charitable purposes? If so, under what circumstances?

Employee Policies

- Hiring—It almost goes without saying that the general employment policy of any company should be to provide equal opportunity for all qualified persons; prohibit discrimination due to race, color, religion, sex, national origin, age or membership or non-membership in any labor organization; and promote the full realization of equal opportunity through a positive, continuing program.
- New employees—Should new employees be hired on a probationary basis? If so, for how long?
- Promotions—Should the company encourage internal promotions when at all possible before seeking outside applicants? Could there be circumstances when this would not be desirable?
- Payroll—Who will be in charge of payroll? How often shall employees be compensated?
- Salary and performance reviews—Which employees will be subject to reviews and how often? How will such reviews be performed and by whom? Will employees be given the right of appeal? Who will judge the appeal?
- Maternity leave—For how long will maternity leaves be granted? With pay? Without pay? What about medical coverage? It should be a firm policy of any management company that all female

employees be allowed to return to their previous jobs with full seniority rights.

- Sick pay—How much time will be allotted annually for sick leave? With pay? Without pay? Should unused sick days be accruable into the following year?
- Bereavement leave—How much leave time will be allotted an employee in the event of the death of someone in the immediate family? What constitutes the immediate family?
- Vacations—Under what circumstances will vacations be granted? How will vacation time be prorated? Should unused vacation time be accruable? Under what circumstances might vacations be canceled and how will the company compensate employees for such cancellations?
- Other office policies—These should include office hours, key control, use of equipment, advertising, leasing commissions, using legal counsel, securing new accounts and time management.

Policies should be incorporated into the everyday operations of the business. When this takes place, they act as guidelines for everyone and there is little need to continually understand the reasons behind them.

Once basic policies are determined, it is prudent for management to prepare a written manual and make sure that every employee has a copy.

THE OFFICE STAFF

An effective and highly supportive office staff is crucial to the success of any property management firm. The size of this staff should be determined by the minimum number of people needed to get the job done. In this respect, look for the number of middle management positions to shrink substantially in the next few decades as lines of authority blur and teamwork becomes more critical.

This having been noted, most property management firms will probably find a minimum of four office employees to be essential: a comptroller, an accountant, a secretary and a receptionist.

Comptroller

In addition to acting as office manager, the comptroller usually is responsible for analyzing and interpreting the bookkeeping records (larger firms may opt to split this function into two separate jobs). This person quite literally controls the day-to-day operations of the company and provides its motivation through leadership, supervision and effective employee interaction. It is vitally important that whoever is selected as comptroller be able to work productively with various types of people.

Accountant

The job of accountant is covered more fully in Chapter 7. This position often has one of the highest turnover rates because its job description is erroneously assumed to include responsibilities and decisions. All good bookkeeping personnel follow established procedures and instructions. An accountant, for example, does not create rates, authorize payments, approve bills or otherwise initiate actions. This is the job of property managers.

Secretary

The position of secretary is one of the most important yet least understood of all jobs, by both employers and would-be secretarial employees. A good secretary, in addition to having basic office skills (typing, preparation of reports, filing, etc.), should be able to perform the responsibilities of two to three full-time property managers when they are otherwise unavailable. This component of the job requires a pleasant personality, common sense and the ability to handle such people as resident managers, owners, contractors and tenants.

In very small property management companies, the role of secretary may often be combined with that of receptionist.

Receptionist

The psychology of professionalism dictates that the receptionist's demeanor reflect the spirit and efficiency of the firm. This is primarily because the receptionist is usually the first company representative that a potential client meets. A company's initial public relations image also depends heavily upon this person. As the cliche goes, "You never get a second chance to make a first impression."

A good receptionist will have a working knowledge of the entire company, including all departments and the role each employee has in them. This person must also have common sense and the ability to use psychology in understanding questions and quickly directing callers or visitors to the appropriate people.

Employees and their job descriptions are discussed more fully in Chapter 5.

A WORD ABOUT EFFICIENCY

The efficiency with which the items in this chapter are dispatched offers clues to keeping administrative costs as low as possible. The proper layout of the office, for example—its equipment, flow, lighting and other fixtures—will keep utility costs down. Keeping reports short and controlling the use of forms will conserve time, as will the use of form letters of standard computerized "boilerplate" paragraphs for correspondence when possible.

Finally, it cannot be stressed strongly enough to use the skills of all your employees to their greatest advantage, presumably the job for which they were hired.

5: Employee Administration

Managers seek to develop and improve the skills of their employees so as to operate the business effectively and efficiently. Specific objectives include

- developing employee policies that contribute to the objectives of the company;
- developing proper procedures for recruiting, screening, placing and training employees as well as establishing proper wage rates; and
- keeping the level of morale and teamwork high.

ABOUT STYLE

Style has been defined as the manner, clarity or character with which we say or do something. Just as there are different kinds of people and, therefore, different kinds of managers, there are different management styles.

One famous example is the story about an angry manager telling his employees, "Buy stock in the Pennsylvania Railroad. I'm going to ship so many of you out that they can't help but declare a dividend."

This is definitely not the way most of us would consider addressing employees. And yet these words were used by a successful and outspoken leader, who was perhaps the best manager in the realm of baseball, Casey Stengel.

Does this story mean that good managers have to frighten their employees into performing well or does it represent a form of psychology? Preferably, we're talking about the latter; employees who need to be frightened to perform well are probably better off in another line of work.

Indeed, an understanding of psychology is basic to the development of a good managerial style. Here are eight important starting points for that development:

1. Be sure of your abilities.
2. Be flexible enough to use those motivational techniques that actually work.
3. Try to understand each employee.
4. Know what benefits and incentives each employee particularly values.
5. Be willing to talk over problems with employees.
6. Be prepared to play actor.
7. Never single out an employee for ridicule in front of a group.
8. Understand the use of timing in implementing any management decision.

MANAGEMENT ATTITUDES TOWARD EMPLOYEES

What constitutes a valued employee? Simplistically, it's one who is performing well. But what does that mean? Two employees can have the same general background and perform the same duties with equal assurance, yet one will be promoted while the other stays behind. Why? The answer says as much about the attitudes of management as it does about those of employees.

Studies have indicated that all employees generally go through four phases or working roles: the newcomer, the colleague, the mentor and, finally, the sponsor. People who build successful careers are those who are seen as passing through all these roles with high performance ratings.

For purposes of this book, only the first two phases (newcomer and colleague) are important; the other two (mentor and sponsor) are management roles.

The Newcomer

The period spent as a newcomer is a delicate time for both manager and employee. This is because good managers are interested in determining how sound a new employee's judgment is, how competently the basic responsibilities of the job are performed and how well things are done.

New employees, on the other hand, must maintain a critical balance between accepting guidance and showing initiative. Too much (or too little) of either can lead to an unacceptable performance rating.

As the manager, you should be interested in personal initiative, but you must also establish clear boundaries.

The Colleague

An employee who successfully completes the newcomer stage rapidly becomes a full-scale member of the team. At this stage, employees are expected to grow. Managers should encourage them to use independent judgment, take an interest in others' abilities and exercise such power and authority as is inherent in the job to be done for the company.

Be aware that a certain amount of stubbornness is at the heart of a good colleague. The trait is a result of self-respect and self-confidence. A responsible colleague gets the job done according to plan, even when opinions differ.

WHAT EMPLOYEES WANT

Work is a major (in some cases, the major) part of life. Indeed, in western civilization, the type of work we do often defines the type of person we are supposed to be. It is little wonder, then, that what goes on at our jobs is also a major topic of social conversation.

Yet, work does not provide the individual satisfaction for many people that it once did. In part, this is because modern businesses are perceived by employees as fostering a worker-bee syndrome. That is, there is the management and then there are the people who actually do the work. In this (alas, all too common) scenario, employees see little need for individual craftsmanship.

Americans find these circumstances particularly irksome because, although they have achieved a high (and enviable) level of choice in both the quantity and quality of goods, they have not attained freedom from preoccupation with economic matters. The result is a paradoxical situation in which many people feel forced to endure jobs they don't like in order to afford a lifestyle they do, without fully appreciating that work is part of that lifestyle. This leads to a mental separation of work and life, the result of which is that success at one's job becomes less important than the perceived success of one's style of life.

As a manager, you should encourage employees to seek personal satisfaction in their work, because employees who enjoy their work are eager, productive and whole. The following, in no particular order, is a list of traits that employees generally feel lead to individual creativity and high job satisfaction.

1. Management maintains an "open door" policy.
2. Employee suggestions, concerns and complaints are eagerly sought and regularly requested.
3. The work is important and not something that can be done by a machine (if the work can be done by a machine, a machine should be doing it).
4. There are five or fewer levels of management (consider that Ford has 17 layers of management while Toyota has five).
5. Communications flow across all levels.
6. Managers emphasize performance rather than status.
7. Independent action is encouraged and rewarded.
8. Mistakes and failures are considered learning experiences.
9. Nonmanagerial employees participate on decision-making committees.
10. There is a profit-sharing or other gain-sharing program.
11. Management works to reduce unnecessary rules and regulations and stresses common sense in policy-making.
12. Management discourages memo-writing in favor of person-to-person contact.

These 12 basic guidelines form the foundation of a good company/employee relationship, that is: loyalty and commitment, personal identification with the company's success and a human relationship between employee and manager.

A Business Philosophy for Employees

Managers can instill in employees a good sense of their worth by starting with an appropriate business philosophy.

1. Have goals and work toward them.
2. Use imagination and think about goals all the time.
3. Act as if it's impossible to fail.
4. Accept responsibility.
5. Speak and write well.
6. Read journals and learn from others.
7. Know company policies and ethical standards.
8. Work with speed, neatness and accuracy.
9. Work with people. Know them by sight and by name.
10. Serve the public through community groups, civic or political organizations or service clubs.
11. Have outside personal interests (hobbies).

A Business Philosophy for Managers

Managers can also instill in their subordinates a sense of their place in the corporate scheme of things by adhering to the following suggestions.

1. Know what subordinates are doing. Make sure they are aware of this knowledge.
2. Ask each employee to have a pet project.
3. Have employees commit themselves to this project.
4. Use deadlines.
5. Have each employee give a seminar on his or her project.
6. Be fair to everyone. This includes people outside your department and the company.

DEVELOPING JOB DESCRIPTIONS

Part of a manager's job is to either hire appropriate employees for his or her area of responsibility or pass on to a personnel department or employment agency a solid list of needed qualifications. This is more important than most managers realize since the fit between a new employee and the job to be done directly affects a manager's ability to get tasks accomplished.

Yet, despite years of analysis concerning what constitutes an ideal employee, fitting people to jobs is almost never an easy task and the decision to hire almost always involves guesswork. The key is intelligent forethought in the development of realistic working job descriptions.

In developing job descriptions, it is best to begin by carefully listing every task that the job entails, including a precise job title and the purpose of the job.

The Complete Job Description

The following is an example of a complete job description as it might apply to a property manager.

Job Title: Property Manager
Purpose: The duty of the property manager is to understand what is happening to the properties under his or her supervision and to:

A. handle reports and budgets;
B. put policies into practice;

C. oversee maintenance;
D. analyze the marketplace; and
E. maintain tenant relations.

General Tasks

1. Inspects the property using an inspection form.
2. Checks the reported occupancy with a personal on-site count.
3. Checks the property for physical problems and deferred maintenance.
4. Reviews the current market and compares it with any problems the property may be having.
5. Reviews tenant problems. Checks for written or photographed documentation.
6. Reviews budgets and operating statements with the resident manager.
7. Checks for accuracy and completion of all tenant-signed documents, including rental agreements and rules and regulations; utility bills; and bookkeeping.
8. Checks that landlord/tenant laws are properly observed.
9. Reviews work schedules of all employees.

Specific Tasks

A. Handling Reports and Budgets
    1. Submits monthly reports to the owner(s) and the management company.
    2. Assists in the preparation of annual budgets.
    3. With the exception of emergencies, obtains company permission for expenses beyond those noted in the budget.
    4. Discusses unusual expenses with the owner(s). Obtains written owner approval for nonemergency expenses not included in the operating budget before the work is performed.
    5. Submits recommendations and justifications for rental increases or reductions to the company.
    6. Periodically reviews the status of the operating budget with the resident manager.
    7. Ensures observance of all federal, state and local laws and compliance with the Federal Wage and Hour Act.
    8. Assumes responsibility for posting all current licenses, permits and notices.
    9. Conducts spot checks of new leases for accuracy and completeness.

B. Putting Policies into Practice

(Although a more in-depth discussion of policies is found in Chapter 4, the following are typical practices expected of property managers and are presented here for guidance and convenience.)

1. Executes responsibility for filling out detailed purchase orders, except for items purchased with petty cash funds.
2. Prepares specific work orders for projects to be performed by outside contractors.
3. Obtains written approval by the account or bookkeeping executive or owner before ordering any contract work in excess of $300.
4. Obtains at least two bids for contract work in excess of $500 and at least three bids for work in excess of $1,000.
5. Ensures that funds are available to pay for contract work.
6. Personally verifies the need for additional supplies and/or services.
7. Ensures that billing statements include work or purchase order numbers and personally approves all bills by initialling them.
8. Reviews receivables, payables and purchase orders to ensure their validity and accuracy.
9. Approves and sends to the accounting department all appropriate invoices for payment as soon as they are presented.
10. Reviews all delinquent accounts and determines the action required.
11. Ensures that all collected funds are transferred to the bank immediately.
12. Periodically audits the petty cash fund.
13. Interviews and hires the resident manager.
14. Discusses annually with the resident manager his or her evaluation of the performance and cost-effectiveness of each employee.
15. Reviews, approves and submits employee time sheets by the date due.
16. Annually reviews all contractual services.
17. Schedules unannounced performance evaluations of all on-site personnel.
18. Ensures that all on-site personnel comply with established policies and procedures.

        19.   Reviews leasing procedures with the resident manager and on-site office personnel.

        20.   Inspects unoccupied or vacant space periodically to determine condition.

C.   Overseeing Maintenance

    1.   Maintains an awareness of energy conservation, implements utility conservation controls and keeps a monthly record of utility consumption.

    2.   Approves the resident manager's work schedule.

    3.   Prepares a daily, weekly and monthly preventative maintenance checklist.

    4.   With the above checklist, inspects at least monthly the interior and exterior of all appropriate structures and prepares written maintenance or replacement recommendations.

    5.   Regularly inspects the completion and quality of all construction, renovation, maintenance and repair work.

D.   Analyzing the Marketplace

    1.   Knows the competition and performs a market survey annually, including vacancy rate comparisons.

    2.   Maintains an awareness of local rent and leasing rates and annually makes recommendations to the management company and owner.

    3.   Recommends an advertising and promotional program.

E.   Maintaining Tenant Relations

    1.   Ensures that tenant complaints get a proper hearing.

    2.   Assists in developing occasional social programs for all tenants of the property.

F.   Addenda

    1.   Executes additional duties and tasks that may be included from time to time as well as variations in the work schedule at the discretion of the company.

    2.   Like all employees, is responsible for adhering to company policies.

Job Skills

The next step is to develop a three-part list of skills necessary for an individual to perform these tasks. Such a list should include:

1. Positively required skills—Examples here might be an M.B.A. degree, a specific number of years of experience with a particular type of property or a willingness to travel extensively.
2. Desirable skills—Familiarity with a particular computer operating system might fit in here, as might experience with property that is of secondary concern to the company.
3. Preferred but not necessary skills—Depending on the job, this could include excellent writing or speaking skills and the proverbial ability to work with people.

Behavioral Characteristics

The above listings, of course, are basically those of education. However, these skills must be matched with a behavior style or personality that will allow the employee to excel in the job. No manager, after all, should be interested in having so-called average workers or workers with poor attitudes on the team.

Behavior, in a nutshell, is how people respond to situations; it is related to their personal value systems. Such characteristics (except at a young age) cannot be taught or changed, and neither are they good or bad.

In general, behavioral characteristics include a person's degree of aggressiveness, sociability or people orientation, level of emotional control or patience and need for a structured environment. Office receptionists, for example, need patience. Accountants usually desire highly structured environments. Managers require sociability.

The question for managers is how well these innate characteristics dovetail with an employee's acquired skills to create an "ideal" employee. The answer, regardless of the number of tests, screenings or interviews you or your company employs, is subjective. How this subjectivity is handled is a prime indicator of judgment, which is, after all, the mark of a manager.

RECRUITING AND FIRING EMPLOYEES

Finding and terminating employees are expensive propositions. The need to fire an employee is often viewed as a failure on the part of a manager to hire an appropriate employee in the first place. And this sense of failure, coupled with the very human desire to salvage a bad situation, often keeps unqualified employees on the job until a real disaster happens.

Where do you find good employees? The first place to look is within the company itself. Encouraging upward movement within the company is an ideal way to retain valuable employees and promote morale, loyalty and teamwork. It also encompasses little risk, in that an employee worthy of promotion is of known quality.

However, even an effective internal promotion program will result in vacancies. As a result it will, at some time, be necessary to consider external recruitment. A general consensus on the effectiveness of external recruitment methods leads us to the following conclusions.

Direct Recruitment: The Best Method.   Direct recruitment of people who are already performing well elsewhere may be viewed as a daring approach, but there is nothing illegal or unethical about this practice in a free-market economy. In fact, an entire sector of the employment agency market—the executive recruitment or "headhunter" firm— does just this.

Referrals: A Good Method.   You can solicit referrals from employees, clients, business associates and friends. There is little need to be concerned that recommendations will be made without regard to qualification. Most people offer referrals only after a great deal of thought, because to recommend an unqualified prospect can damage a reputation (and, in some cases, a friendship).

Employment agencies also fall into this category, although they must be chosen with care and provided with a detailed job description.

Classified Advertising: Another Productive Method.   This can yield good results with a minimal expenditure of time if you can screen prospects from their letters and resumes. Remember that every ad creates an image for your company and that, if you wish to attract the best prospects, the ad should be as positive as possible.

Employee Applications

Traditionally, employment applications serve three purposes: to screen out unqualified prospects, to provide information for an interview and to obtain references. In general, a good application form is also designed to assist in judging behavioral characteristics as well as job skills.

Typical questions asked on such forms include the following:

1. Personal information (name, address, social security number, etc.). Beware of asking questions that do not relate to job performance. Such questions include, but are not limited to, age, race, sex, religion, ethnic origin and marital status. If such concerns are pertinent (i.e., the prospect is a family man and the job

entails a lot of out-of-town travel), they are best brought up during the interview.

2. Education and special training.
3. Employment history.
4. Health (as related to job performance).
5. Credit references (as indicators of behavior and stability).
6. Legal concerns.
7. Outside interests (hobbies, memberships in professional or civic organizations, etc.).

The employment form should be simple and direct and ask only those questions that can be easily verified. In this respect, questions of health, credit and legality (i.e., arrests/convictions) can be verified only upon the written consent of the prospect.

The major reason to check into a prospect's employment history used to be to confirm experience and productivity. However, legal concerns now make it difficult for former employers to provide (either in person or in writing) any but the most basic of information. A carefully conducted interview is vital, therefore, in determining whether an applicant has the qualities and experience you need.

Finally, remember that common courtesy, corporate image and good business sense require that all letters and applications for employment be acknowledged as quickly as possible.

The Interview

From management's point of view, an interview has only one real purpose: to obtain sufficient information so that a decision can be made on whether or not to hire someone. From a prospective employee's point of view, it is (or should be) to determine the company's attitude toward people and the work to be done. Therefore, all questions and discussions that take place at this time should address these two points.

Because an interview is an oral exchange in which subjective information is also being sought, it is best conducted in a comfortable environment. Also, as an open and free exchange of information is being sought, it is prudent not to conduct an interview too quickly, although the actual time will vary depending on the job to be filled.

While techniques vary, there are several steps in conducting any successful interview.

1. Make sure that the interview is conducted by the manager who will actually do the hiring.

2.   Before you conduct an interview, study all available information about the prospect, including the employment application. In addition, review the job specifications and list of behavioral characteristics.
3.   Don't ask questions that require simple "yes" or "no" answers. Obtaining insight into a person is a complex matter that requires not only appreciating what is said, but what is unsaid.
4.   Begin by asking open-ended or broad questions that allow the prospect to choose his or her approach and discuss the matter in terms of what is important to him or her.
5.   Gradually narrow the questions to specific points of fact.
6.   Ask all job applicants the same questions so that you can evaluate their responses fairly.
7.   Be prepared to answer questions that the prospect should bring up. Encourage such questions, if necessary. This is an important matter in your decision to hire; the kinds of questions a prospect asks are clues to knowledge, professionalism and behavior.

Finally, once you have made your decision to hire, move quickly, as the market for skilled workers is always competitive. Figure 5.1, the New Employee Information Report, will help speed the paperwork.

Terminating Employees

You will have only two reasons for terminating employees: adverse financial conditions and unacceptable performance. Individual corporate financial problems are beyond the scope of this book. But what constitutes unacceptable performance? The answer to this question can have grave legal consequences.

Unacceptable performance is cloaked in the legal terminology of *just cause*. In general, just cause for terminating an employee can be found in three areas: (1) moral turpitude; (2) complaints; and (3) violation of licensing laws.

It is possible to understand the effects of the last two points as they pertain to the business of business. Determine what constitutes moral turpitude, however, can be extremely challenging. Whenever you have more questions and concerns than facts, seek legal guidance.

Be aware, however, that failure in a task, or even a series of tasks, does not necessarily qualify as unacceptable performance or just cause for termination. Indeed, the toleration of failure is a particular attribute of successful, positive and innovative management firms. In addition, the possibility of failure is implied in any plan and in any decision.

Figure 5.1   New Employee Information Report

Property: _____   *Date:* _____

Prepared By: _____

Name:	
Social Security Number:	
Address:	
Birth Date:	Marital Status:
Effective Date Of Employment:	Position:
Monthly Salary/Hourly Rate:	
Person To Notify In Case Of Emergency:	
Relationship To Employee:	
Address:	

The Following Forms Must Be Attached:

Employment Application	
Form W-4	
Form I-9	
Employment Agreement (if applicable)	
Bonding Application	
Group Insurance Enrollment Card (if applicable)	
Personnel Status Change	
Sample For Business Card Printing (if applicable)	
Request For Credit Cards (if applicable)	
Others: _____	

Check Licenses Employee Holds:

Real Estate—Sales		Contractor: _____	
Real Estate—Broker		Dealership: _____	
Notary Public		Other: _____	

Remarks: _____

_____

_____

Instructions:
1. To be completed as needed.

If the employee violates company policies or has otherwise performed unacceptably at less than termination-serious levels, consider filing (and make sure the employee knows you are filing) an Employee Reprimand Report (see Figure 5.2).

If it is determined that there is just cause to terminate an employee, it is vital that an Employee Exit Report (Figure 5.3) be filed and all final paperwork and compensation be completed immediately.

PERSONNEL DEVELOPMENT AND MOTIVATION

Part of management's job is to promote good employer-employee relations so as to establish a productive, interdependent, long-term association. Without such a relationship, there can be no sense of loyalty or team spirit.

There are only three basic actions that any manager need do to instill loyalty and spirit: (1) promote morale, (2) inspire confidence and (3) encourage personal and professional development. Getting more specific, we can break this down into the following practical considerations:

- Promote morale through orientation for new employees; constant and effective communications; and salary reviews and bonuses.
- Inspire confidence through personal projects and promotions.
- Encourage personal and professional development through continuing employee education.

New Employee Orientation

There is no excuse for not properly initiating a new employee into the company. This oversight is counterproductive from an economic standpoint, in that the employee is left to his or her own devices to discover who's who and what's what and why. It is also disheartening to the point that many new employees find themselves silently asking, "Why am I here?"

After incurring the expense of hiring a new employee, it is foolhardy not to formally welcome him or her to the company with an appropriate orientation program. Such a program need not be time-consuming, although some companies, such as Walt Disney, take as many as four days to orient each new employee.

Chances are, of course, that your management firm is not as large or diverse an enterprise as Disney and it may only require half a day or so to accomplish the same goal. All good orientation programs, regardless of the company type or size, are designed to give new employees a sense of their place in the scheme of things and an understanding of what is expected of

Figure 5.2   Employee Reprimand Report

Property: _____   *Dàte:* _____

Prepared By: _____

Name:	
Employee Number:	
Oral:	Written:
Nature Of Reprimand:	
Employee's Signature:	
Supervisor:	

Instructions:
1. This report should be completed on an as-needed basis.

them. This is accomplished by explaining the company's philosophy and operating methods. The following list is a good example of what should be covered:

- the company's history, successes and objectives;
- the management style;
- how each division relates to other divisions and to the company's overall objectives, with special emphasis on where the new employee fits into the structure;
- terms of employment, such as hours, pay schedules, holidays, benefits and services, etc.;

Figure 5.3 Employee Exit Report

Property: _____ *Date:* _____

Prepared By: _____

Name: _____

Address: _____

_____

Position: _____

Salary: _____

Hired Date: _____

Termination Date: _____

Reason For Termination: (Check and explain)

_____ Laid off due to lack of work   _____ Discharged, fired

_____ Voluntary quit   _____ Other

Explanation: _____

_____

Recommended For Re-employment?

_____ Yes   _____ No

Final Check:

Number of days worked	_____ days @ _____	= $ _____
Overtime pay	_____ hrs. @ _____ × 150%	= $ _____
Accrued vacation days	_____ days @ _____	= $ _____
Severance pay	_____ days @ _____	= $ _____
Other	_____ days @ _____	= $ _____
Gross Amount Due		$ _____

Keys Returned?	_____ Yes	_____ No	
Credit Cards Returned?	_____ Yes	_____ No	
Insurance Conversion?	_____ Yes	_____ No	

Forwarding Address: _____

_____

Comments: _____

_____

_____

Instructions: To be completed by the interviewer before employee leaves the company.

- a general discussion on policies and rules, particularly as they affect public relations, personal attitudes and the future (if these are extensive, a handbook should be made available);
- a detailed explanation of the job that includes a discussion of the employee's systems support, that is, where help is available; and
- a tour of the company and personal introductions.

Communications

The importance of keeping employees informed has been noted earlier in this chapter (see the section "What Employees Want"). Of 12 concerns, three (that's 25 percent) deal with communications. To restate:

- communications flow across all levels;
- nonmanagerial employees participate on decision-making committees; and
- management discouraged memo-writing in favor of person-to-person contact.

However, good employee morale is the result of more than strictly work-related communications. Remember that work is also a human enterprise and that morale is a result of attitude. A solid company "team" or "family," therefore, sponsors activities outside the realm of work. The idea here is that the company should express personal appreciation or concern.

It does not necessarily take a lot of effort to show that a company values its employees, but, as most people in the property management business are highly intuitive, it does take sincerity. Such sincerity can be demonstrated by several kinds of extra attention. For example:

- Bowling leagues, picnics or other such events are always good morale builders. Having the company pick up the tab, buy an extra round or provide an unexpected or unannounced surprise is a show of sincerity.
- Likewise, appreciation dinners are good examples of sincerity. They might include small presents for each employee (and not with the company logo on them), gag gifts specifically (and tastefully) attuned to each employee's best idiosyncrasy or baby-sitting services.
- Personal expressions of sympathy or hospital visits. Extra attention here would include gestures by management in addition to an employee's immediate supervisor.

- Granting emergency or personal time off. Very few employees will ever abuse this privilege and most will be grateful if it is granted without strings (i.e., lost pay, guilt, etc.) and in a gracious manner.

Again, the idea to express is that an employee is appreciated, wanted and valued as a member of the company. Remember that grateful employees are assets and will return company sincerity many times over.

Salary Reviews

Effective communication at all levels is not a cure-all for many management concerns. The need for adequate compensation, in the form of money, cannot be glossed over.

This is because money is much more than the means by which we buy things. Although it is easy to equate (or delude ourselves into equating) money with greed and the need to accumulate things, in truth, the real value of money is not that simple.

Money, by itself, has no intrinsic value. It is strictly a cultural symbol of worth. Unlike most other symbols, however, we can hold it in our hands and express worth through its use. Thus, money is the tangible guide by which worth is gauged.

No amount of communication (because it is an intangible) can take the place of adequate monetary compensation. It is never an employee's fault if he or she leaves the company to earn more money elsewhere. In a free-market economy, there is nothing ethically or morally wrong with seeking to maximize one's worth. This is as true for businesses as it is for individuals and is, in fact, one of the cornerstones of our economy.

Salaries should, therefore, be reviewed at least annually. Reviews should take into consideration national as well as local trends, as modern technology makes it just as easy to move across the nation as across town.

In determining the salary compensation for a property, you will need to know:

1. The degree of skill that the property manager possesses now.
2. How many units (or buildings and their type and location) the property manager is taking care of.
3. The property manager's goals with the company. Is money the prime consideration or is prestige (i.e., benefits such as a company car, etc.)?
4. The general salary and compensation ranges, not just for property management, but for allied industries as well. The following figures represent overall national averages:

Base salary: Minimum to sustain lifestyle
Percentage of fee: 20–27 percent
Listing commission: 25 percent
Sales commission: 25 percent
Finder's fee: 50 percent of first month's management fee

Occasional cash bonuses are also ideal morale builders, especially when an employee has performed beyond standards or everyone has worked especially hard to make a plan work. Such compensation should be made as soon as possible to reinforce the achievement. Also, beware of awarding bonuses that are very large, as they rapidly become political and just as rapidly discourage other employees. On the other hand, don't award an employee who has just saved the company a quarter of a million dollars with a check for $100.

One final word on bonuses: regular annual bonuses have their place if they are tied to the performance of a division or the company. As a general rule, however, such bonuses lose their impact because they are expected. Bonuses serve their purposes best when they are unpredictable and/or intermittent.

Closely allied to monetary compensation in today's economy are fringe benefits. Due to rising taxes on income, such benefits are often vital inducements to both initial and long-term employment. Such benefits as paid holidays and vacations are fairly standard. Stock options and the use of a company car are valued by long-time employees, as are retirement plans. Health and dental care plans, especially for employees with families, are absolute necessities and day-care services are increasing in importance.

A new trend is to offer flexible plans that allow employees to select their own fringe benefits from a menu of choices. Regardless of the arrangement chosen, management should review such benefits as often as it reviews salaries.

Pet Projects

Allowing an employee to pursue a personal project is not only an ideal confidence builder, but also often leads to a more productive operation. Such projects also keep an organization flexible, innovative and in the marketplace.

Often, however, employees won't have such a project in mind. As a manager, you should be aware of the tendencies, biases or inclinations that every employee has and be prepared to "volunteer" a particular someone (with his or her permission, of course) when a special concern arises.

Keep in mind that in allowing employees to pursue personal projects, you are not just expressing confidence, but are allowing them to grow professionally. While this practice may result in a burst of behavior that is disconcerting at first, let the creative process run its course. Just keep in mind that there is a difference between creativity and innovation. Creativity is the ability to think up new things. Innovation is the ability to make those new things work. Your role as manager, therefore, is to make sure that the road to innovation is not hindered. This attitude will bolster your employees' confidence and allow them the necessary luxury of feeling a part of the team.

Promotions

As noted in a previous discussion, promoting people from within is important to developing positive company spirit (see Figure 5.4). Few things damage employee confidence more than seeing someone from outside the firm hired for a job that could have been filled internally.

Employees who know that they have a real opportunity for advancement constantly prepare themselves to assume more challenging roles. Don't assume, however, that everyone wants to move up. Some employees, especially relatively new ones, may find themselves more interested or better challenged by jobs that require lateral moves.

Continuing Employee Education

Maintaining professionalism requires that all employees have the opportunity to learn new skills and develop new talents. Long-time employees, especially, need to maintain their competitive edge in rapidly changing times. It behooves management, therefore, to either establish formal, ongoing, organized training programs or encourage employees to attend outside seminars and classes that serve similar purposes. Likewise, employees should be encouraged to become members of professional organizations.

To encourage participation in outside programs, management should consider defraying their cost if they are completed successfully. This practice also makes an excellent fringe benefit.

APPRAISING PERFORMANCE

Because managers generally are responsible for setting goals, it is essential for both the company and employees that managers formally appraise individual performance (Figure 5.5). This requirement is in addition to the daily appraisals managers inherently make.

As successful performance can only be measured in the context of goals, however, it is first important to review what was expected of employees in terms of specific, identifiable and obtainable objectives. Incidentally,

Figure 5.4 Personnel Change

Property: _____ *Date:* _____

Prepared By: _____

Name:	
Employee Number:	
Address:	
Type Of Change:*	
From:	
To:	
Rate From:	
Rate To:	
Seniority Date:	
Effective Date:	
Comments:	
Employee's Signature:	
Supervisor:	

Instructions:
1. This report should be completed on an as-needed basis.

*Type of change: New Hire, Termination, Rate Change, Vacation Request, Address Change, Transfer, etc.

Figure 5.5   Employee Appraisal Form

Employee Name _____ *Position* _____

I. Job Duties/Key Responsibilities
Comments:

II. Goal Achievement
Comments:

III. Major Accomplishments/Contributions Not Part of Goals
Comments:

IV. Performance Behaviors
Comments:

V. Areas Requiring Modification/Development
Comment:

VI. Overall Rating (Circle)
OUTSTANDING   ACCOMPLISHED   NEEDS IMPROVEMENT

VII. Summary of Overall Performance
Comments:

_____   _____
Signature of Appraiser   Date

---

do not confuse the obtainable with the easy. Effective goals should be challenging. Also, all goals must have been communicated to employees and agreed to before the appraisal. In short, the essential task of an appraisal is to compare what was accomplished with what should have been accomplished.

Appraisals are required in four common situations: work guidance, career guidance, salaries and promotions. You may have other reasons also, but appraisals must always have well-defined purposes based on relevant and accurate information. Keep in mind that because all appraisals are matters of opinion, they should be made as honestly as possible with every opportunity for individual employee input (and right of appeal) before any final decisions are made.

6: Marketing Administration

Marketing a property management company presents many unique challenges, but none is more important than convincing a prospective client that placing his or her investment property in your company's care represents a prudent investment decision. This kind of effort demands a carefully planned, multifaceted presentation.

Use the information gathered in developing your business plan (see Chapter 3) when you put together your presentation. Then your marketing effort is not only specifically targeted to the appropriate economic and demographic base, but also is designed to offset the effects of competition (i.e., why us and not them).

KNOW WHAT THE CLIENT EXPECTS

You can begin to appreciate the marketing effort by reviewing the criteria that a prospective client will look for in a property management firm. Although the specifics will depend on your particular field in the local marketplace, such criteria will generally include:

I. Company and Personnel Information
    A. Overall experience of the company and the personnel who will be responsible for supervising, managing and leasing.
    B. Accreditation by or membership in industry trade groups, such as the Institute of Real Estate Management (IREM), National Apartment Association (NAA) and Building Owners and Managers Association (BOMA).

II. Services
    A. Ability to provide timely administrative support services,

accounting reports and payroll services for on-site personnel.

B. Ability to provide all other necessary property management services (e.g., budgeting, tenant relations, rent analysis, marketing programs, etc.).

III. Experience
   A. Specific management experience involving the type and location of the property to be managed.
   B. Leasing experience involving the type of property to be leased and its particular market area.

IV. Current Business
   A. Projects currently being managed and/or leased.
   B. Disclosure of current business that would compete with the prospective property or other conflicts of interest such as ownership in maintenance firms.

V. Fees
   A. Fee structure and amount, plus the estimated costs of on-site and off-site personnel (to be borne by the owner).
   B. Third party fee management experience.

VI. Other
   A. Written policies and procedures for preventive maintenance programs or for the procurement of services and supplies.
   B. Positive business and credit reference checks.
   C. Experience in managing distressed properties and foreclosure takeovers.
   D. Ability to provide space planning, engineering, construction supervision, energy conservation and other services with experienced in-house personnel.
   E. Insurance in place to protect against crime or loss.

DEVELOPING THE MARKETING APPROACH

In light of these expectations, it is first necessary to appraise your company's ability to qualify or compete for a new account. Once this capability is satisfactorily established, you can develop the actual marketing approach, which should be based on the so-called Five P Program: *Preparation, Presentation, Price, Promises and Policy.*

Preparation

As a general rule, prospective clients will want to visit your place of business. The general appearance of your office, therefore, makes an important statement about your attention to professionalism. It makes sense to invest in making the company's business location as presentable as possible. This phase should include landscaping and signage as well as attention to cleanliness and neatness.

Presentation

There are two aspects to presentation: the face-to-face meeting and advertising or public relations.

The Face-to-Face Meeting. In order to perform this function, the manager must:

- *Know the Management Company's Background.* There's an old salesforce adage to the effect that you can't sell what you don't know about. If you are to be a good manager, you must understand your company's total business, including its age, size, services, types of properties under contract and number of clients.
- *Like the Company for Which You Work.* An important corollary to the above adage is that you also can't sell what you don't believe in. You must truly believe that your company is the best one for the prospective client.
- *Know the Local Market.* Be aware of what's happening, including all new construction, changes in traffic patterns and new zoning ordinances. Keep files of newspaper clips (by subject and/or area) and specifically track costs, types and vacancy factors of rental properties as well as the cost of site-built and apartment housing.
- *Know the Competition.* Conduct a regular survey to determine the strengths and weaknesses of the competition relative to your own company.
- *Know the Prospective Client.* It's important to know as much as you can about the prospective client before you meet face-to-face. How many properties does he or she have? Why do you think this prospect might be in the market for a new property manager? Have other property managers caused problems in the past? Are there specific problems with the property?
- *Address the Basic Concerns of the Prospect.* Develop a formal or informal presentation that presents your company's services and abilities in a logical manner. It is important that this presentation

Figure 6.1 The Client Presentation Outline

Topic	Subjects To Be Discussed
Company Introduction	• Accreditation • Background
Company Personnel	• Experience • Certification

Services Provided	• Partial Listing
	   Rent Collection
	   Bill Payment
	   Reports
	   Maintenance
	   Tenant Relations
	   Other Factors

Benefits to Client	• Partial Listing
	   Identify Cost-Effective
	      Activities
	   24-Hour Emergency Service

Existing Clients	• List Clients • Photographs of Currently Managed Properties
Forms and Reports	• Copies of Most Used, Unique or Special Reports

be flexible enough to address the specific needs of the prospective client. Figure 6.1 can serve as a basic presentation outline. Consideration should also be given to the relative merits of a completely live presentation (usually high, but only if done by a good public speaker) versus the use or partial use of video (expensive but effective if done well) or slides (less expensive than video, easier to customize, but more awkward to handle).

• *Listen to What the Potential Client Has to Say.* Many people love to talk. A real professional listens and responds to what he or she hears. In this respect, always maintain a positive outlook so that you help good potential clients make the decision to sign a contract. But never make a deal unless you know for certain that you can make it work to everyone's satisfaction (see the section "Promises," below).

Advertising and/or Public Relations. An effective marketing strategy captures a prospective client's interest. Once this interest is determined, techniques can then be developed for displaying your strategy. As a general rule, this strategy will be based on a sense of value, which is defined as economy (i.e., price, amenities, etc.), service and/or prestige. Knowing what the competition is doing is mandatory here.

An important marketing technique is to display strategy through the development of a theme, that is, a unifying symbol or phrase. This is a common business practice. As of this writing, for example, unifying themes include Ford Motor Company's "Quality is Job 1," and American Airlines's "Something Special in the Air." These phrases express the underlying philosophy of the company as it attempts to distinguish itself in the marketplace. Such themes should be part of a good graphics system and used on all communications, including signs, stationery, business cards, brochures, ads, company vehicles, newsletters and so forth.

The most common techniques for attracting prospective clients involve the use of signs, brochures, direct mail, publicity and public relations efforts, referrals, canvassing and display ads that include *Yellow Pages* and other directories. Each has advantages and disadvantages, and your use of them will be determined by your own strategy.

- *Signs*—All signs, whether they are used for promotion, directions, identification or information, should be posted in prominent but appropriate positions. Promotional and informational signs should direct questions to either the company's overall business manager or a specific individual. As inquiries from signs usually come by phone and letter rather than in person, make sure that the sign includes the company's name, address and telephone number.
- *Brochures*—Contrary to general belief, brochures and other similar materials function primarily as useful reminders rather than introductions. Therefore, they are best presented after a contact has already been established. A good general brochure should describe company features in terms of service benefits and provide useful information that may not be appropriate to discuss during a first visit (see Figure 6.2).
- *Ads*—Large display ads in major metropolitan newspapers and especially in business or trade magazines/newspapers can effectively reaching a select audience over a wide area. Classified advertisements, however, rarely market a company effectively.
- *Direct mail*—This can be the quickest method through which to gain clients. The irony here is that such a marketing technique addresses those not actively looking for a change. But it is precisely these prospective clients who are most likely to be responsive to

Figure 6.2 Sample Contents of a Property Management Company Brochure

1. History of the company
2. Property management/brokerage relationship
3. Starting date and term of contract
4. Property management fee calculations
5. Use of budgets and forecasts
6. Responsibility of the management company
7. Qualifications of the company staff
8. Sample property management agreement
9. Sample monthly operating statements
10. Properties managed
11. Bank and other references

offers for better value, service and/or location (see Figures 6.3, 6.4 and 6.5 for sample letters).

- *Public Relations*—Many otherwise good property managers do not understand what public relations (PR) is. The general goal of public relations is to create, through the organization of news, events and advertising, an advantageous opinion on the part of the client. The most common form of public relations is the news release. Other forms include parties and special events to announce a new service or an involvement by the company in an important community matter. The success of a public relations plan rests on a good idea, a thorough execution and something that adds a dash of emotional appeal. However it is devised, a well-executed public relations program can be a cost-effective supplement to other marketing techniques.
- *Referrals*—Recommendations by current, satisfied clients are a powerful tool with a high ratio of success. If you gain a client through a referral, always be sure to find out who it is and send a note of thanks (offer a referral fee and/or a dinner invitation if appropriate). It's good public relations.

Price (Fees)

It should always be your intent to get the maximum fees possible for the services your company provides. This will not necessarily be the same as charging the highest possible fee, because the value of a service is a matter of perception and will vary from client to client. A good method upon which to base the value of a particular service is to conduct a comparison study of fees charged by other property management companies.

Figure 6.3   Sample Letter for Sales/Condominium Management

Dear _____:

Nurturing and sustaining the growth of certain properties is the direct result of an effective maintenance and marketing program. A professional property management program can, in fact, prove invaluable to the protection and appreciation of your investments. Our firm can provide such a program to you at a competitive cost.

Our research indicates that your complex is using a sales/leasing program originally created by the developer but that may not necessarily be serving your current needs. Our firm will manage your property with the overall mission of protecting each homeowner's investment and acting as the guardian of the value of your property. Our goals are to:

1. satisfy the needs of homeowners and investors;
2. develop an overall management plan;
3. keep costs in line with budgeting; and
4. provide an open line of communications between the board, homeowners and our company.

We understand the management needs of properties like yours and we would like to send you a bid proposal for our services. Such a bid would cover three service options: full service management, leasing and sales.

Full service management would cover (but not be limited to) all bookkeeping, banking and record procedures as well as the handling of liens, attorney relations, attendance at meetings, notice mailings, the enforcement of rules and regulations and all maintenance concerns. Of course, all work would be done in accordance with the instructions of the board.

A *leasing program* would follow the practices set forth by the State Real Estate Department and the Landlord/Tenant Act. In the matter of a *sales program*, our firm is a licensed brokerage.

I have taken the liberty of enclosing additional information about our firm, including a brochure, references and brief resumes of our company's officers and associates.

We recognize that each client has unique requirements and that a truly effective management plan should be personalized to those needs. Therefore, I would like to discuss your requirements with you and ask for the opportunity to present a proposal at your earliest convenience.

Yours truly,

Figure 6.4   Sample Consulting Proposal and Agreement

Date:

To:

Subject: Marketing and economic feasibility study regarding a possible
                    mobile home park on the client's 40-acre site.

Background: The owners have a 40-acre parcel under consideration for
                    development as a mobile home park.

Introduction: The owners approached this firm to obtain the required
                    professional expertise needed to produce this study.

Scope of Work: The requirements of the study may include all or part of the
                    following:

1. Determine the general market for mobile home parks in
   the general geographic area.
2. Evaluate the competition:
   a) By general location.
   b) By occupancy factors.
3. Review proposed location:
   a) Attractions/advantages.
   b) Disadvantages.
   c) Per status of nearest competition.
4. Develop cost factors:
   a) Improvement costs.
   b) Projected operating/financing costs.
5. Calculate pro forma financial statements based on:
   a) Costs.
   b) Projected market capture.
   c) Seasonal variations.
6. Provide conclusions about marketing feasibility.
7. Make recommendations regarding:
   a) Phased development.
   b) Promotion and business development.
   c) Financial packaging.
   d) Effective management.

Cost: Not to exceed $75.00/hour or $500.00/day.

Accepted: _____   _____
                          by Owner   by Consulting Company

_____, the client, hereby authorizes the work outlined in the
above PROPOSAL to be completed for the sum stated.

_____
        Signature—Company Name

Date: _____

Figure 6.4   Sample Consulting Proposal and Agreement (continued)

```
_____ , as consultant, hereby agrees to perform the
assignment detailed in the above PROPOSAL for the sum stipulated.


                          _____
                                  Consultant Signature

          Date: _____
```

Promises

Keep all promises (including "deals") to prospective clients within reason, and you will be able to keep all promises.

Policy

The basic policy of all marketing programs is that the rules of operation apply uniformly to all clients.

THE BASIC MARKETING PROGRAM

The previous discussion contained references or allusions to items covered in Chapter 3, "Starting the Management Firm." Much, if not all, of the information needed for an effective marketing program should be available from a properly prepared business plan. The following 10 questions—the answers of which should be in the business plan—summarize the important points to be addressed in this area.

1. Where is the market?

2. Where is the market going?

3. Where are we today?

4. Where do we want to be in five years?

5. How much will it cost to get there?

6. What are the strategic (major) risks?

7. What are the obstacles?

8. Who are the competitors?

Figure 6.5   Sample Letter for Property Management

Dear _____:

   It was nice meeting with you and discussing property management for
_____. This property is an excellent facility,
and you and the owners should be proud of it.
   The marketing problems you are now experiencing are very similar to
those I have solved on other occasions, and I am confident that they can be
resolved to your satisfaction. Along with the normal property management
services our firm will provide, I personally will devote my full effort toward filling
this property with qualified tenants in the least amount of time possible.
   Before any successful marketing effort can be attempted, a thorough
understanding of the property is necessary. This will come about during the
"take-over" procedure outlined below:

1. Set up the property.
    a) Review operating budgets from preceding years.
    b) Write letters notifying all tenants and vendors of new
        management.
    c) Verify insurance coverage.
    d) Process all other account and administrative items necessary to
        set up a new account.

2. Inspect the property.
    A checklist is used for a comprehensive first look at the property to
    determine its physical status.

3. A management plan will be written for review by you and the owners
    with recommendations as to the direction the property manager
    should take. This plan will include:
    a) Review of income:
        1. Rents.
        2. Vacancy.
        3. Other income.
    b) Review of operating expense.
    c) Marketing survey.
    d) Major repairs and replacement requirements (if any).
    e) Capital expense requirements (if any).

   In order to develop the marketing plan, the in-depth marketing survey
(c, above) is very necessary. This will bring to light sufficient data to provide an
understanding and assessment of the market area and will allow us to develop
innovative and aggressive marketing strategies.
   With the management plan and the marketing survey as tools, we can
develop an effective marketing plan. This plan will be divided between (1) a
conventional marketing approach and the implementation of (2) innovative
marketing ideas.

Figure 6.5 Sample Letter for Property Management (continued)

     The conventional marketing approach would utilize advertising, public relations and the hiring of market-oriented, experienced on-site managers, in addition to a close monitoring of the project. While the need for this cannot be overemphasized, innovative marketing avenues will be continually explored.
     Therefore, as part of our fee, we will provide you with the following:

1. a management plan within one month;
2. a marketing plan within two months;
3. complete supervisory management;
4. relevant reports on a timely basis; and
5. consultation services as needed.

Our management fee will be the greater of:

1. Five percent (5%) of the first $35,000/month effective gross income and three and one-half percent (3.5%) of effective gross income over the initial $35,000, OR
2. $800.00 per month.

     Enclosed is a copy of the property management agreement. Please review it and, if you have any questions, don't hesitate to contact me.

Sincerely,

---

9. Where are the competitors going?

10. What payoff do we expect?

     Be aware that because times and circumstances change, the marketing plan you first develop will probably need to be modified at some point. It is fundamental, therefore, that the plan be flexible. In general, such a marketing plan should be divided into three major steps and set out as follows:

1. Gather information (review business plan).
   - Determine target clients. (Who do you want to do business with?
   - Determine competitive activity. (Who is already doing business in your market area and how are they doing it?)
   - Determine the objective of the marketing program. (What will set your business apart from your competition?)

- Determine the program's strategy. (How will you illustrate these services and abilities? Will you use a video or slide presentation?)
- Determine the budget.

2. Establish corporate identification.
    - Develop a company image (logo, slogan, etc.), based on program strategy, for use in all marketing media (brochures, signs, business cards, etc.).
    - Be active as a good community citizen.
    - Keep existing clients. It's far better (and, frankly, easier) to assure the satisfaction of existing clients than to continually look for new ones.
    - Know and work with professionals from other related businesses (bankers, lawyers, etc.) as well as civic and government organizations (Chambers of Commerce, planning commissions, etc.)
    - Use marketing tools: publicity, sales aids (brochures, etc.), direct mail, etc. Don't forget existing clients.

3. Manage the marketing program.
    - Analyze cost-effectiveness on a regular basis.
    - Be prepared to change the program as conditions change or new opportunities present themselves.

MARKETING THE NEW BUSINESS

Marketing a new property management company, which starts well before the business opens its doors, involves three basic steps: developing the marketing plan (above), pre-opening details and the opening day program.

Approximately a month before opening, furnish information about your business to local media such as newspapers and influential organizations such as the Chamber of Commerce. This information, in the form of a press release, should include the location of your business, the general size of your company (if appropriate), the years of experience (and names) of the principals and the types of properties you will be specializing in, along with the names of some of the better-known clients/properties you already have.

Opening day is a good time for public relations as well as a reason to celebrate. Both of these objectives can be accomplished by having a party. Just be sure that, in addition to staff, family and friends, you invite current clients, business associates (including Chamber of Commerce personnel), your banker, your lawyer, construction contractors and anyone else who either helped in starting the business or could help bring in new clients.

MARKETING THE OPERATING BUSINESS

Competitive business surveys should be a fact of corporate life. Conduct one annually in order to keep abreast of your company's position in the market. In addition, it is very important to learn from any failures to gain new business. A letter and survey to prospective clients who have rejected your services (Figure 6.6) should be a tool of your marketing plan.

Only as your ability to provide management services approaches a saturation should you consider phasing out part of the marketing program in favor of improving operational efficiency. This is not say that marketing programs can be completely eliminated. Keeping a company positioned and well known in the marketplace is a constant challenge, and the outline in Figure 6.7 should be considered in one form or another.

MANAGING A PROPERTY MANAGEMENT
MARKETING DEPARTMENT

In a classic marketing story, a heated discussion occurs between a marketing manager and a company president, who is standing beside a map with multicolored pins that indicate sales in particular areas. "My advice to you," says the president, "is to take the pins out of the map and stick them into the salespeople."

Inevitably, this is where any marketing plan succeeds of fails, with the ability and enthusiasm of its sales force in carrying out the plan. And the responsibility for that rests with the marketing manager (or whoever has volunteered or been assigned to handle that role). Such duties in this area can be divided into two major functions: (1) developing an effective marketing force and (2) planning and controlling the marketing effort.

Developing an Effective Marketing Force

A marketing manager must know how to select, train and compensate a marketing force. The selection of qualified people should be handled in the same manner as any prospective employee, starting with the development of a job specification (see Chapter 5). Training must include not only information on the company background and its services and performance record, but also its specific new accounts policies and procedures (including terms of payment) and mock presentations. In this regard, new marketing

Figure 6.6   Follow-up Letter and Survey

Dear (Prospective Client):

Recently, our firm bid a property management contract that you had made available to us. It has always been our concern that all our clients receive the best that can be offered. However, to paraphrase Robert Burns, "If we could see ourselves as others see us. . . ."

It would be very much appreciated if you could assist us in this matter. Please take a few minutes to answer the accompanying list of questions. Just mail the survey back to us in the self-addressed stamped envelope.

Thank you for your assistance.

Sincerely,

(name)

CONFIDENTIAL
COMPANY PRESENTATION—REVIEW AND ANALYSIS

1. Did our staff respond quickly to your initial inquiry?   Yes _____   No _____

2. Were our employees courteous and informative?   Yes _____   No _____

3. Was the literature on the company prepared clearly and factually?   Yes _____   No _____

   Comments: _____

   _____

   _____

4. Was our review of your project thorough?   Yes _____   No _____
5. Was the quoted management fee too high?   Yes _____   No _____
6. Was the presentation by our staff thorough and professional?   Yes _____   No _____
7. Were all your questions answered to your satisfaction?   Yes _____   No _____
8. What were your reasons for not choosing our firm?

   Comments: _____

   _____

   _____

   _____

Figure 6.6   Follow-up Letter and Survey (continued)

9. Please be specific in any other comments you may have concerning how
    we could improve our services.

    Comments: _____
    _____
    _____
    _____

people should always accompany experienced ones for a certain length of
time.

Unfortunately, there is no single plan for motivating or compensating
a marketing force. A sound plan must be fair and reasonable, relatively simple and economical. It must be based on factors over which the marketing
force has some control, but must prevent large payments during times of
high business activity at the expense of low payments when adverse conditions prevail. This is primarily because times of adversity are precisely when
you need an effective marketing force the most, and low compensation will
drive that force elsewhere.

A general breakdown of compensation among property management
companies for such a force is as follows:

- 50 percent provide a salary plus an incentive.
- 25 percent use a salary plus a bonus.
- 25 percent offer straight salaries.

Planning and Controlling the Marketing Effort

A marketing manager should be, first and foremost, a property manager, if only to understand and appreciate the challenges involved. In addition, he or she must also be a good office manager, with all skills that
implies, including people skills. To make any marketing effort work requires
the cooperation of the entire company's staff (including onsite personnel).
The best plan in the world won't work if (1) no one believes in it and/or (2)
no one believes in the person presenting it.

In developing the plan, the marketing director should have an open
line of communication with upper management in order to discuss ideas
and ensure that goals are realistic and acceptable to the principals.

Figure 6.7   Marketing the Operating Company

I. **PURSUE POSITIVE WORKING RELATIONSHIPS WITH:**
   A. **Real Estate Community:**
      1. Pay full commission to brokers.
      2. Mail letters wherever necessary.
      3. Sponsor professional seminars/sponsor lectures.
      4. Prepare detailed fact sheets on company.
      5. Present seasonal (or special reason) gifts to key people.
      6. Hold one-on-one breakfasts/lunches.
      7. Become involved in special events (sports, etc.)
      8. Publish a quarterly corporate newsletter

   B. **Other Opinion Makers in the Community:**
      1. Lenders.
      2. Corporate facilities leaders (e.g., economic developers, etc.).
      3. Give thanks/Do:
         a) Seasonal/holiday greetings.
         b) Direct contacts.
      4. Keep a master list—follow up.

   C. **Tenants/Clients in Buildings Presently Managed:**
      1. Quality newsletter.
      2. Updates of manager memos.
      3. Personal visits.
      4. Sponsorship of an annual social event.

II. **CONTINUOUSLY MARKET A TEAM EFFORT**
   Always remember that marketing is a team effort; it should involve everyone in your firm as well as those associated with your firm, including lawyers, accountants and consultants. Consider the following approach:

   A. Direct Mail to Specific Prospective Clients.
   B. Good Corporate Brochure.
   C. Fact Sheets.
   D. Corporate Video.
   E. Slide Presentation.
   F. Architectural Models/Renderings of Properties Managed.

To control the marketing effort, plans must have specific, measurable goals and objectives that can be tracked and analyzed for effectiveness as the program is unfolding. If a public relations or advertising firm is hired, the marketing manager should provide guidance and direction and ensure that every item developed is consistent with the marketing approach and theme.

KEEPING EXISTING BUSINESS

It is always easier to keep a client than to get a new one. One way to keep your current clients happy is to communicate with them on a regular basis—not just when you're sending them financial reports. Consider providing the following:

- Copies of inspections
- Newsletters and annual reports
- Newspaper clippings
- Photos of the property
- Letters/birthday cards
- Phone calls
- Holiday gifts
- Dinner/gift certificates
- Tickets to sporting/cultural events

When in doubt, it is always best to ask directly what the client desires, such as a five-year budget or more detailed reports. Gifts should always be considered items of appreciation and, as such, should never be so expensive as to be construed as anything else.

Regardless, the entire company—not just the property manager assigned to the client—must help in this marketing effort.

BE INNOVATIVE

While the ultimate value of a property management marketing plan is measured by the speed with which it succeeds, remember that it takes time before the effectiveness of most plans is apparent. A plan's success will depend somewhat on the imagination and creativity it shows. A good marketing manager, therefore, must be willing to take risks by trying something new or approaching something from a new perspective. This is especially true in an area with steep competition. Don't be afraid to consider new ideas in marketing your company.

7: Financial Administration

Five functions are basic to good financial administration: planning, controlling, financing, costing, and miscellaneous management. General definitions are as follows:

Planning is the process of deciding on future actions.

Controlling is the ability to use the resources of the company efficiently and effectively so as to accomplish the goals planned. This includes the actual accounting procedures, budgeting and reporting.

Financing is ensuring the availability of funds. This involves not only raising funds, but also investing them.

Costing deals with fee determination and the actual cost of doing business.

Miscellaneous management includes such things as tax and pension management, computer operations and forecasting.

THE ACCOUNTING FUNCTION

It is important to distinguish between accounting and bookkeeping. Bookkeeping is the nuts and bolts of systematically recording money transactions in their proper places (i.e., keeping the books). Accounting, on the other hand, is a system of using the information in these books to analyze the financial position and operating results of a business. The word comes from *account,* which is to explain, justify or consider.

Sound accounting procedures that result in clear, concise financial reports, therefore, are the most important part of a management company's duties. Ironically, the world's most efficient financial reporting system will not be a marketing advantage, because property owners expect good, up-to-date reports. The value of such systems is to the management company, because of the time that can be involved in preparing such reports, time that could be better spent managing properties.

Basic bookkeeping requires that separate records, supported by documentation and prepared in accordance with generally accepted accounting principles, be maintained for each property (see Chapter 8 for a more comprehensive look at this area). The management company must provide control over these books and records so as to protect the owner's assets from theft, negligence or fraudulent activity, including:

- Theft of assets by management company employees
- Losses due to delayed payment or invoicing
- Overpayment of costs arising from fraud or error
- Unauthorized use of facilities by management company employees

THE OPERATING SCHEDULE

Figure 7.1 is a general schematic for the flow of financial work. As a rule, the management company is responsible for furnishing reports that sum up all transactions for each property during the previous 30 days (see Figure 7.2). These reports should be submitted within 10 to 15 calendar days after the close of each month. Copies of the reports must be sent to the property owner(s), filed at the management company and available for government inspection.

These financial reports, which can vary depending on the specific management agreement, usually include such items as collections, delinquencies, uncollectible items, vacancies, summaries, projections and estimates.

Supporting documentation, which must be available upon request, includes general ledger listings, invoices, copies of paid bills, the rent roll, bank statements and detailed cash receipts and disbursement records. (See Appendix B for an in-depth accounting operations manual.)

REPORTS TO OWNERS

The two basic financial statements provided to owners are the balance sheet (Figure 7.3) and the profit and loss statement (Figure 7.4).

The balance sheet indicates the overall financial condition of each property at a specific time. Money in each account is summarized by category.

Figure 7.1   Financial Schematic

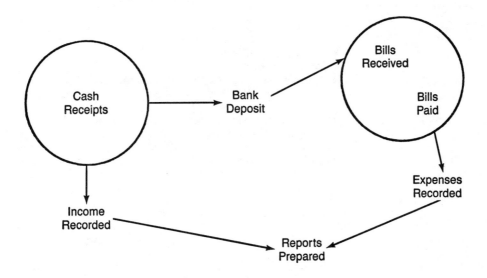

The profit and loss statement shows results for the stated period of time and, if desired, can also provide comparative data for previous periods. Revenues and operating expenses are listed separately by account number.

REPORTS TO THE GOVERNMENT

Payroll Reporting

As a general rule, withholding taxes (including FICA) are sent to the government monthly, depending on the amount of undeposited taxes. Quarterly forms that are submitted to federal and state taxing authorities reconcile the tax liabilities with actual deposits.

Unemployment Tax

Although unemployment insurance is a federal-state system, each state, as well as the District of Columbia, Puerto Rico and the Virgin Islands, has its own law and operates its own program. As such, the amount paid by each employer is determined by the state and may be increased or decreased depending on the number of claims. An experience rating form

Figure 7.2   A Typical Operating Schedule

Date of Month	Activity
1st through 5th	• Rents due on all properties. • Mail out mortgage payment. • Process incoming bills and prepare check requests. • Bank reconciliation with computer and check register.
6th through 10th	• Close out for previous month in the computer. • Print computer reports. • Print checks to the 18th of month. • Mail out late notices or late charge notices. • Print out delinquency report.
16th through 20th	• Mail out sales tax report. • Print out checks to the end of the month.
25th	• Prepare following month's check request for mortgage payment.
30th	• Mail all journals from on-site locations to the home office.

NOTE: A procedure for handling client and management company accounting, as well as certain common accounting forms, can be found in Appendix B.

from the state is usually sent to businesses to notify them of any changes in the state unemployment tax rate.

Federal unemployment taxes are accumulated and deposited at the end of each quarter if total undeposited taxes exceed $100.

Property Tax

If applicable in your state, this tax may be collected and paid by the company handling the debt service (i.e., mortgage, etc.).

Rental Tax

If applicable, the rental tax is paid regularly (usually monthly) to the state and/or local government. It is based on paid gross receipts for each property in question.

Figure 7.3   Sample Residential Property Balance Sheet

ASSETS		
Current Assets		
Cash	$ 20,000.00	
Total Current Assets		$ 20,000.00
Property and Equipment		
Land	$ 600,000.00	
Building	75,000.00	
Building improvements	20,000.00	
Office furniture	500.00	
	$ 695,500.00	
Less Accumulated Depreciation	(45,000.00)	
		650,500.00
Total Assets		**$ 670,500.00**
LIABILITIES AND CAPITAL		
Current Liabilities		
Current portion of long-term debt	$ 10,000.00	
Accrued wage and related taxes	150.00	
Accrued expenses	100.00	
Total Current Liabilities		$ 10,250.00
Long-term Debt, Less Current Portion		445,050.00
Owner's Capital		215,200.00
Total Liabilities and Capital		**$ 670,500.00**

Personal Property Taxes

Personal property taxes may not apply in your state. If they do, they cover property other than land and buildings (i.e., furniture, fixtures and other equipment). These items are depreciable for tax purposes and should be listed as they are purchased. The state and/or local government will send you a bill indicating how much tax is owed and when it is due.

REPORTS FOR THE MANAGEMENT COMPANY

A property management company must maintain scrupulous financial records of all transactions and other business conducted on behalf of

Figure 7.4   Sample Residential Property Profit and Loss Statement for Year-to-Date
Ended October 31, 19XX

	CURRENT MONTH			YEAR-TO-DATE		
	Actual	Budget	Variance	Actual	Budget	Variance
Revenue	$14,544	$14,000	$ + 544	$95,500	$90,000	$ + 5,500
Expenses	(7,195)	(6,500)	(695)	(51,125)	(46,500)	(4,625)
Net Operating						
Income	**$7,349**	**$7,500**	**($151)**	**$44,375**	**$43,500**	**($875)**
Debt Service	(2,436)	(2,436)	0	(24,360)	(24,360)	0
Cash	**$4,913**	**$5,064**	**($151)**	**$20,015**	**$19,140**	**($875)**

NOTE: Several items in this report will require explanation: revenues (up by $544), the increase in expenses (up by $695) and the year-to-date cash flow (down by $875).

clients. These records are vitally important not only to the clients, but also to the financial health of the management company itself. A clear distinction must be made between the expenses and income made on behalf of clients and those of the management company, especially at tax time.

Two types of expenses must be accounted for: (1) those that are reimbursable by the client and (2) those that must be borne by the company as costs of doing business. Of course, in a strict sense, all company expenses must be paid for through client fees, and Figure 7.5 offers a representative breakdown of those that are client billable and those that must be paid for through company profits.

FEES

Property management fees are based upon terms in the management agreement. These terms may be a percentage basis (e.g., 5 percent of gross revenues), a flat fee regardless of revenues, cost-plus or some combination of the others.

Fees can also be collected for leasing services, repairs and alterations, tax appeals and other services such as appraisals, special reports or maintaining the property's books (see the section "Special Fees," below).

Fees should not be collected on items not directly associated with revenue generation. This category includes security deposits, rebilling of utilities, tenant reimbursements, the sale, refinance or condemnation of property and insurance proceeds. Figure 7.6 is an example of a billing statement for appropriate fees and reimbursable expenses.

Figure 7.5   Representative Accounting Costs

Reimbursable
- Service contract agreements
- Collections through a third party
- Legal fees (including violations) pertaining to a property
- Certain capital requirements
- Printed checks
- Leasing commissions
- Property advertising
- Printed forms and supplies
- Telephone, postage and other special items
- Property repair costs

Nonreimbursable
- Salaries/benefits of management company employees
- Accounting services
- Basic supplies and forms
- Computer costs
- Training expenses
- Company advertising expenses
- Insurance costs
- Political and charitable contributions
- Overhead and general expenses
- Costs of branch offices
- Basic capital expenses

THE BREAKEVEN CHART

Profit is, of course, one of the two major determinants of the fee structure (expense of providing the service being the other). In this regard, the Breakeven Chart (Figure 7.7) is valuable for determining the point at which a profit can be made.

The Breakeven Chart provides a graphic illustration of the relationship of expenses and revenues to profit. The following six steps are used to construct such a chart:

1. The horizontal base line (also called the X axis) can represent either the total ability of the management company or the capacity of property being managed. The unit of measurement can vary. For an industrial or commercial property, for example, this line might represent the percentage of total square footage. In a retail or residential property, it might be percentage of units. For a management company, it could be the percentage of the total number of properties that can realistically be managed.
2. The vertical line (Y axis) represents expenses in terms of dollars.
3. A horizontal line, parallel to the base or X axis, represents all fixed costs.
4. Where the line in 3, above, meets the Y axis is the starting point of the total cost line. Total cost is the sum of the fixed and variable costs.

Figure 7.6   Fees and Reimbursable Expenses Billing Statement

Property: _____   Prepared By: _____

Date: _____

1. Monthly Management Fee $_____

2. Reimbursable Payroll Expenses

Title	Full/Part-Time	Salary (Monthly/Hourly)	Benefits (Insurance/Fringe)	Sales Taxes
_____	_____	_____ per_____	$_____	$_____
_____	_____	_____ per_____	$_____	$_____
_____	_____	_____ per_____	$_____	$_____

Accounting Costs (if any): $_____ per_____

Payroll Service Cost (if any): $_____ per_____

Total Payroll Expenses: $_____

3. Other Expenses Paid by Management Company (description):

_____

_____

Total Other Expenses: $_____

4. Other Reimbursable Services (construction, supervision, etc.):

Service	Compensation
_____	$_____
_____	$_____
_____	$_____

Total Other Services: $_____

5. Incentive Fees: $_____

TOTAL MONTHLY BILLING (Add totals of 1, 2, 3, 4 & 5): $_____

Figure 7.7   Breakeven Chart

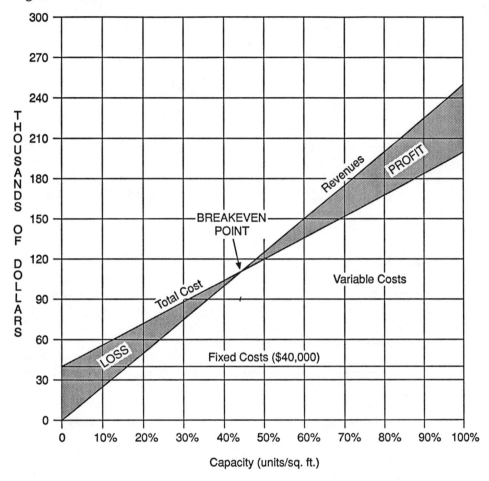

5. The revenue line is drawn starting at the zero point at the lower left of the chart.
6. The breakeven point is where the total cost line crosses the revenue line. The area to the left represents loss. The area to the right represents profit.

In the example shown in Figure 7.7, the breakeven point occurs when costs and revenues intersect at a figure of approximately $100,000. To achieve this, approximately 45 percent of the total capacity of the property must be rented. Because of the chart's graphic nature, it becomes obvious that the breakeven point can be altered by reducing the variable costs and/

or raising revenues. How much this can be changed depends on the property and local market conditions.

While the Breakeven Chart provides a visual analysis, the following formula provides the same information:

$$Breakeven = \frac{Fixed\ Costs}{(Revenue - Variable\ Costs)}$$

Regardless of which method is used, the information is invaluable, not only in determining fees for a management company or a particular property, but also in evaluating the economic viability of an individual property in the first place. As such, it should be used in the decision to take on a property or client.

DETERMINING COSTS

Fixed operating costs should be reduced to the lowest denominator per month for the properties being managed (e.g., units, square footage, etc.). In this manner, a basic initial fee can be determined regardless of the individual property and/or client.

In the following example, it is assumed that the XYZ Property Management Company, which specializes in residential properties, manages 6,500 units.

XYZ MANAGEMENT COMPANY OPERATING COSTS

Salaries and Benefits	$250,000
Travel and Entertainment	10,000
Office Rent and Equipment	100,000
Supplies and Telephone	75,000
Professional Services	50,000
Other Expenses	35,000
Interest Expense	7,000
Total Annual Fixed Expenses:	$527,000
Per Month (divided by 12):	$ 43,917
Per Unit (divided by 6,500):	$6.76

Based on fixed expenses of $527,000 annually (the fixed cost line), this company must charge a minimum of $6.76 per unit per month. To this must be added certain variable costs, which are inherently tied to the number of properties being managed. These costs include inspections, consultations, supervision, special meetings and reports and other circumstances. It is not unusual for these variables to double the initial fixed cost figure.

Because most variable costs for a management company involve personnel, the following list represents average hourly charges that should be considered as of this writing. Be aware that actual figures may be higher or lower depending on local economic conditions.

Personnel	Hourly Rate	
President	$50.00	
Property Manager	$50.00	
Construction Site Manager	$30.00	
Maintenance Foreman	$15.00	
General Repair	$20.00	
Clerical Research	$12.00	
Gardener	$10.00	
Plumber	$24.00	
Delivery/Pickup	$10.00	(plus mileage @ 20¢ per mile)

These figures represent rates charged above fixed costs, but they can also be used when determining a fixed fee to be charged (i.e., fixed costs). Figure 7.8, a general budget listing, can be used to determine fixed operating expenses as well as current net income or profitability.

SPECIAL FEES

Depending on your capabilities and desires, your management contract may include provisions for fees for services outside the realm of normal management operations. Examples of such services and fees would include:

Startup Fees

Startup fees are required to set up initial records and property examinations. For small apartments and commercial office buildings of up to 20,000 square feet, for example, the average current fee should be $500 to $2,000. For commercial office space of up to 75,000 square feet, current rates are $750 to $2,500.

Figure 7.8   Management Company Operating Income and Expenses

Account Code	Income	Amount
4001	Property Management—Residential	$ _____
4002	Property Management—Shopping Centers	_____
4003	Property Management—Office/Industrial	_____
4004	Property Management—Other	_____
4010	Leasing Commissions	_____
4020	Other Income	_____
	TOTAL GROSS INCOME	$ _____
	Expenses	
5101	Salaries	$ _____
5120	Bonuses	_____
5170	Worker's Compensation	_____
5171	Payroll Taxes	_____
5172	Group Insurance	_____
5180	Other	_____
	TOTAL SALARIES AND BENEFITS	$ _____
5301	Transportation Costs	$ _____
5302	Meals	_____
5303	Lodging	_____
5304	Auto Mileage Allowance	_____
5306	Auto Leasing	_____
5308	Other	_____
	TOTAL TRAVEL AND ENTERTAINMENT	$ _____
5501	Office Rent	$ _____
5502	Office Equipment	_____
5503	Depreciation	_____
5504	Repairs and Maintenance	_____
5505	Security	_____
5506	Other	_____
	TOTAL OFFICE RENT AND EQUIPMENT	$ _____

Figure 7.8   Management Company Operating Income and Expenses (continued)

Account Code	Expenses (continued)	Amount
5601	Telephone	$ _____
5602	Answering Service	_____
5603	Office Supplies	_____
5604	Printing	_____
5605	Postage	_____
5606	Mailing Service	_____
5607	Other	_____
	TOTAL SUPPLIES AND TELEPHONE	$ _____
6001	Professional Services	$ _____
6002	Legal	_____
6003	Data Processing	_____
6004	Accounting	_____
6005	Other	_____
	TOTAL PROFESSIONAL SERVICES	$ _____
6010	Bank Charges	$ _____
6102	Charitable Contributions	_____
6103	Gifts	_____
6104	Licenses/Permits	_____
6105	Memberships/Dues/Subscriptions	_____
6106	Seminars	_____
6107	Advertising	_____
6108	General Insurance	_____
6109	Social Functions/Meetings	_____
6110	Other	_____
	TOTAL OTHER EXPENSES	$ _____
6201	Interest Expense	$ _____
	TOTAL OPERATING EXPENSES (All Expense Totals + Interest)	$ _____
	NET OPERATING INCOME	$ _____

(Total Gross Income – Total Operating Expenses = Profits)

Renovation, Maintenance and Construction

Not included in the basic contract and at the owner's request, the fees for renovation, maintenance and construction are usually based on a percentage of the accepted bid and include site management as needed. Current average fees vary from 20 percent for small apartments and commercial offices of up to 20,000 square feet, to 18 percent for structures of up to 75,000 square feet to 15 percent for residential buildings and condominiums.

Late Rent or Bill Collection

It is not unreasonable for a management company to add a charge of 5 percent of any late fee for acting as a collection agency. This charge, of course, depends on the terms of the lease.

Leasing Commissions

If your management company is also acting as the property's leasing agent, then it is wise to consider fees based on the length of the negotiated lease. For leases of up to five years, such a fee is typically 5 percent of the total rent.

For leases of five through 15 years, typical fees are 5 percent of the total rent for the first five years, plus 2.5 percent of the total for the remaining ten years.

For leases with terms of more than 15 years, consider 5 percent of the total rent for the first five years, 2.5 percent of the total for the next ten years plus 1 percent of the rent for the balance of the term.

Consulting Fees

Calculations of hourly consulting fee and similar charging must take into consideration not just the cost of the person acting as consultant, but also the overhead of the entire company. The general formula is that a consulting fee equals the cost (salary) of the consultant plus the cost of company operations plus a profit.

The following example represents a typical calculation based on our previous example of XYZ Property Management Company.

1. Annual Cost of Company Operation (ten employees) = $527,000
2. Calculation of Productive Hours per Employee
        40 hours × 52 weeks   = 2,080 hours/year

less 15 days vacation
and 6 days sick time $\quad = \quad \underline{240 \text{ hours/year}}$

Total Hours per Employee $\quad$ 1,840 hours/year

3. Calculation of Productive Hours per Staff

$1,840 \times 10$ employees $\quad = \quad$ 18,400 hours/year

4. Calculation of Company Operating Costs per Hour

$\$527,000/18,400 \quad = \quad \$28.64/\text{hour}$

5. Calculation of Consulting Fee

Salary of Consultant $\quad = \quad \$50.00/\text{hour}$
Company Operations Cost $= \quad \$28.64/\text{hour}$
Total $\quad = \quad \$78.64/\text{hour}$
Profit (10 percent) $\quad = \quad \$\ 7.86/\text{hour}$
Total Consulting Fee $\quad = \quad \$86.50/\text{hour}$

Other Fees

The following is a detailed list of additional fees that may be available for consideration.

- Notary public
- Market research
- Space planning
- Teaching/Seminars
- Appraisals
- Late charges
- Signage
- Credit checks
- Lockouts/Evictions
- Brokerage
- Tax appeals
- Vending machines
- Transfers
- Sublets
- Photocopying
- Forms costs
- Brochures
- ID Badges
- Management training
- Day care
- Inspections
- Construction management
- Conversions/Tenant improvements
- Parking garage operation
- Accounting
- Lease service
- Key charges
- Painting
- Public relations
- Refinancing
- Income tax preparation
- Applications
- Referrals
- Insufficient funds
- Postage
- Advertisement placement
- Storage
- Towing
- Grant and proposal writing
- Expert witness

COMPANY BUDGETS

Budgets are best thought of as the working tool of management because they require managers to give planning top priority. Such plans can then be formalized through the definition of goals and objectives, which serve as benchmarks for evaluating performance. As an early warning system, budgeting also uncovers potential problems.

Budgeting provides a vehicle for communicating these plans in an orderly way throughout the company, coordinating activities and ensuring that the plans and objectives are consistent with the broad goals of the entire organization.

A good budget is an itemized estimate of income and expenses for the future. In developing a budget, perform the following steps:

1. Determine the probable level of revenue.
2. Determine which operating expenses are fixed and which vary with revenue. In general, almost all expenses for a management business should be fixed.
   - Fixed expenses should be expressed in dollars.
   - Variable expenses should be expressed as a percentage of revenue and then transferred to dollars in the budget (e.g., for a management fee of 5 percent of revenue, multiply .05 times revenue).
3. The budget period is usually set to correspond with the fiscal year.

In the complex, everyday course of managing client properties and developing and analyzing client reports, it is easy to forget that you must treat your own company as Client Number 1. For your property management company to survive, you must exercise the same care and expertise accorded to other clients on behalf of your own business. This must include the use of breakeven analysis, profit and loss statements and especially budgeting. These tools coordinate the activities of the entire company, uncover potential problems before they occur and provide benchmarks for evaluating company performance. Use them.

8: Overview: Issues of Property Administration

Although the focus of this book has been the development and operation of a property management company as a business, this chapter examines traditional property management activities that influence efficient business operations. In this respect, this chapter is a link between the operation of a property management business and the business of managing properties. The specifics of managing particular properties are covered in numerous other publications.

Indeed, the management of properties must start in the company's business office if that function is to be performed in compliance with the management plan.

MAJOR MANAGEMENT SERVICES

To appreciate the administrative aspects of your clients' properties, review the major management services that are generally offered to clients regardless of the type of property (see Figure 8.1).

You must provide these services, in turn, in a systematic manner. Here, Figure 8.2 illustrates the basic property management organization that should be incorporated or taken into account in developing the overall business structure.

Next, the day-to-day operation of any property should start with the establishment of a master information list of important names and phone numbers (Figure 8.3). Such a list should be available to property managers in a standard form at the main business office. If it is later customized with a property schematic on the reverse side (or attached), the list can quickly provide information necessary to resolve problems.

Figure 8.1   Major (Basic) Management Services

ACCOUNTING

- Monthly operating reports (income and expenditures).
- Budget analysis.
- Rent analysis.
- Collection services (rent, billing, delinquencies).
- Bank account maintenance.
- Bill payment.
- Tax and other government report filing.

EMPLOYEES

- Establishing work schedules.
- Hiring, orientation, training and supervision.

LEGAL

- Compliance with all building, fire and other government codes.
- Negotiation and monitoring of all service contracts.
- Monitoring and enforcement of leases, rules, regulations and policies.
- Arranging for employee bonding.
- Verification of contractors' insurance policies.

OPERATIONAL

- Property inspection.
- Preventive maintenance.
- Monitoring of electrical and mechanical systems.
- Prompt handling of all tenant requests/complaints.
- Supervision of security programs and personnel.
- Supervision of grounds maintenance/unit turnovers.
- Inventory maintenance.
- Marketing the property.
- Administration and supervision of recreation programs.

GENERAL

- Supervision of all tenant construction.
- Provision of timely management reports.
- Provision of and adherence to an approved management plan.
- Securing appropriate insurance and processing all claims promptly.
- Regular communication with owners and tenants.
- Attendance at all required meetings.

POLICIES FOR PROPERTY MANAGEMENT

You will also need to develop and adhere to a set of policies and procedures for the day-to-day management of properties. While these policies are not to be confused with the office policies noted in Chapter 4 and referred to in Appendix A, they must not conflict with them either. In short, the

Figure 8.2   Organizational Chart

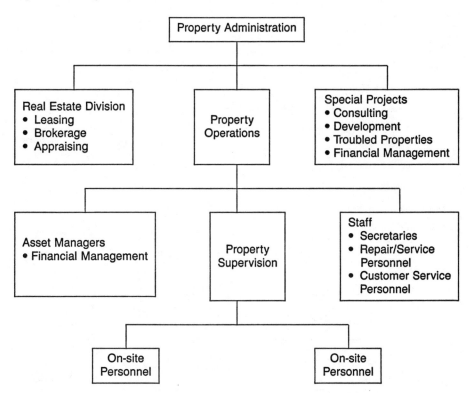

policies (procedures, etc.) developed to run the property management company must be reviewed when setting up policies to operate an actual property. To do otherwise can, at the very least, lead to employee and management confusion. At worst, it can pave the way to ethical and, perhaps, legal challenges.

The specific property policies needed will depend, to a great extent, on the type of property being managed. A mobile home park in the suburbs, for example, will require different leasing policies than will a high-rise building downtown. In general, however, we can arrange the need for property policies into the following areas:

Legal
- Landlord relationships
- Evictions
- Rental applications

Figure 8.3   Property Information Sheet

Property: _____ Date: _____

Prepared By: _____

Location: _____ Property Number: _____

_____

Number of Units: _____ Property Phone Number: _____

Management Agent: _____ Phone Number: _____

Manager: _____ Phone Number: _____

Assistant Manager: _____ Phone Number: _____

Maintenance Chief: _____ Phone Number: _____

Security: _____ Phone Number: _____

Fire Dept.: _____ Phone Number: _____

Police Dept.: _____ Phone Number: _____

Pool Service: _____ Phone Number: _____

Other: _____ Phone Number: _____

Fiscal Year: _____

Insurance With: _____ Expires: _____

Insurance Agent: _____ Phone Number: _____

Checking Account Bank: _____ Acct. No.: _____

Savings Account Bank: _____ Acct. No.: _____

CONTACTS AND/OR OWNER(S)			
Name	Address	Home Phone	Work Phone

INSTRUCTIONS: To be completed at the purchase of a new property and updated annually or as needed.

- Ethics
- Zoning and permits
- Licensing
- Fair housing
- Miscellaneous (e.g., pets or waterbed agreements)

Insurance
- Tenant insurance
- Property damage claims
- Liability claims
- Hazard elimination

Management
- Job descriptions
- Public responsibilities

Maintenance
- Safety and security
- Energy conservation
- Planning and scheduling
- Inspections
- Work orders/complaints
- Emergency procedures
- Inventory
- Appearance
- Equipment

Marketing
- Telephone usage
- Greetings/tours
- Client/tenant qualifying
- Rent schedules
- Surveys
- Traffic reports
- Occupancy reports

On-site Office
- Employees

- Filing
- Communications

Tenant Relations
- Tenant transfer
- Tenant selection and acceptance
- Handling violations
- Social programs
- Tenant associations
- Leases
- Rules and regulations

On-site Accounting and Reporting
- Reporting timetables
- Audit procedure
- Rent collections
- Records maintenance
- Fees
- Chart of accounts
- Non-sufficient funds
- Payroll/time cards
- Pegboard/computer use
- Approvals
- Bank deposits
- Property personnel expense reports
- Hiring
- Budgeting
- Billbacks

As previously noted, the actual development of property policies is a subject best left for property-specific management publications.

THE PROPERTY OPERATING BUDGET

Chapter 7 described certain aspects of fiscal reporting and fee determination within the context of developing appropriate techniques for corporate financial administration. The success of these techniques will be reflected in the ability of your company to manage properties, not merely supervise them. It is this function, management versus supervision, that determines the efficiency of each property's operating budget.

An operating budget is concerned only with those cash items of income and expense that are anticipated during the coming year. The difference between an operating and a stabilized budget is that the latter is an estimate of projected figures for a number of future years and takes into account any reserves for the replacement of capital items.

The operating budget is, in essence, the working management plan for a property, a plan distinct from that of every other property the company is managing. As with any aspect of effective planning, this budget is created by (1) establishing reasonable goals in a timely manner with the adequate participation of all those concerned, (2) developing a flexible procedure to achieve those goals and (3) auditing the results of the procedure on a regular basis and in cooperation with those who helped establish the goals.

The Income Stream

Space rental is the major source of income, and it is always the marketplace that will determine the price. In seeking to establish a rent schedule, start by pricing the best unit in the complex and adjusting the price of the others accordingly. The definition of the word *best* will also be determined by the marketplace in the form and number of amenities that renters consider important. These amenities may include

- view (including balconies and patios);
- decoration (e.g., carpeting, drapes);
- public facilities (e.g., swimming pool, tennis courts, restaurants, recreational areas, etc.); and
- services (e.g., parking, delivery, doormen, etc.).

The additional price of such amenities may have to be revised based on comparable properties, the age of the property and its general aesthetics.

If certain available public facilities and services are not included in space rental, then these become potential sources of other income. Such sources can include

- parking;
- storage;
- laundry;
- moving;
- vending machines;
- cleaning services;
- pet services/charges;
- fax/copying/mailing services; and
- health clubs.

Income figures will not be consistent, but will vary as market conditions dictate. Nevertheless, the overall annual income figure should be in general agreement with the budgeted amount.

In planning the final operating budget income figure, be sure to distinguish between gross rental income and adjusted (or effective) gross rental income.

Gross rental income is the amount of money that may be taken in under ideal conditions. *Adjusted* (or effective) *gross rental income* takes into account probable losses in income due to anticipated vacancies, move-out and move-in delays, credit losses and bad debts. An operating budget must always be based on the adjusted gross rental income.

Operational Expenses

Property expenses can be broken down into eight general categories:

1. Payroll
2. Utilities
3. Maintenance
4. Insurance
5. Taxes and licenses
6. Advertising
7. Management
8. Other (supplies, professional fees, service contracts, etc.).

In listing such expenses, include only those items that are actually expected to be paid during the budgeted year.

Preparing the Budget

In general, a prepared property budget utilizes the following outline:

1. Gross rental income (GRI) $ _____
2. Cost of vacancies, etc. $ _____
3. Adjusted GRI (1 − 2) $ _____
4. Other income $ _____
5. Adjusted gross income (3 + 4) $ _____
6. Operating expenses $ _____
7. Net operating income (5 − 6) $ _____
8. Capital expenses $ _____
9. Financing costs $ _____

10. Cash flow (7 – 8 & 9) $ _____
11. Monthly income to owners (10 ÷ 12) $ _____

Actual money figures can be stated as percentages of gross rental income, a practice that allows you to compare budgets with those for previous and future years as well as with budgets for comparable competitive properties. Figure 8.4, for example, presents a sample operating budget for a medium-sized apartment complex. Figure 8.5 compares expenses with gross rental income (other income not included) as percentages in pie-chart form.

PROPERTY BUSINESS PLANS

Financial constraints may require that you develop a property-specific business plan for financial institutions or investors. Such a plan (Figure 8.6) will use elements originally noted in the development of the management company itself, as discussed in Chapters 1 (e.g., the management plan outline) and 7. In addition, information will be needed on leasing, commissions, the cost of "free" rent, vacancy costs and tenant improvement costs.

REPORT WRITING

Given the nature of the business, property managers write a lot of reports. But whether it's a management report, marketing survey or an entire management plan, certain principles of documentation apply. These principles involve (1) determining the facts needed, which will lead to (2) the method by which these facts will be gathered.

Any report calls for one or more of five types of facts:

1. *Historical data* involve company, property and/or industry background. This includes management attitudes, philosophy and past decisions.
2. *Projections,* which use historical data for reference, include objectives, anticipated expansion and insight into future expectations.
3. *Current procedures* detail current operations, including the flow and frequency of work and the integration of employees.
4. *Cost analysis* looks at such items as salaries and personnel, rent, purchases and inventories.
5. *Effectiveness* data examine such items as the advantages and deficiencies of procedures, adequacies for future expansion, the usefulness of records and reports and possible duplication of effort.

Figure 8.4   Apartment Complex Sample Operating Budget

INCOME	
Gross rental income	$120,000
Losses due to vacancies, bad debts, etc.	10,000
Adjusted gross rental income	$110,000
Other income	15,000
Adjusted Gross Income	**$125,000**
EXPENSES	
Gross salaries and other compensation	$ 20,000
Real estate taxes	12,000
Utilities (listed separately)	2,500
Supplies (listed separately)	300
Contract services	3,000
Repairs (minor)	750
Repairs (major)	1,000
Insurance (listed separately)	500
Management (5% of adjusted gross)	6,250
Legal, accounting, other administrative	450
Total Expenses	**$46,750**
Net Operating Income	**$78,250**
Capital expenses	16,000
Financing costs	32,000
Cash Flow	**$30,250**
Monthly Income to Owners/Investors	$2,521.83

Because there is always a tendency to expand the scope of a report, the largest concern in gathering data is to limit the details to those actually required. Standardized forms can be of great help in this matter when the facts required are brief (as in financial statistics, dates, names, addresses, etc.). In matters of analysis, however, using forms may not always be possible. Here, two methods of gathering facts can be employed to keep things on track:

1. *Secondary research* is a means of gathering existing facts by examining current documents and records. Secondary research should not be viewed as inferior to primary research, because it is often a necessary prelude to understanding current trends.

**Figure 8.5   Apartment Complex Expense Analysis Based on
Gross Rental Income (GRI) Only**

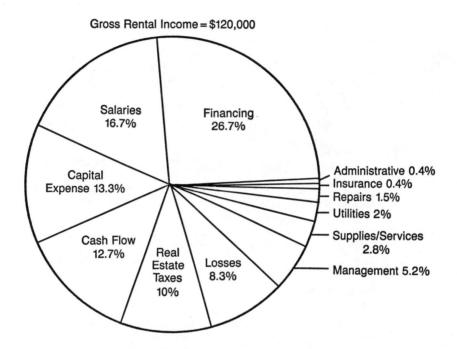

2. *Primary research* involves the gathering of facts or opinions that are not now known. Primary research techniques generally involve the use of questionnaires and interviews. In both cases, use extreme care in the planning and wording of questions. There should be some means for checking into discrepancies between what is being done and what some party says is being done.

Market Surveys

Just as you undertake a market survey as part of the company business plan (Chapter 3), it is vital that you also survey the marketplace at least annually for the property or properties being managed. These surveys, while written for the owners, provide the basis for effective management and keep your property management company apprised of overall market conditions, the knowledge of which is vital to your own continued success.

Figure 8.7 outlines a typical property market survey. Although conclusions and recommendations are listed first, this is for efficiency of time

Figure 8.6   Property Financing Plan Outline

A. Discussion
  1. Description of the property.
  2. Type of business property, historical data, etc.
  3. Comparison with competition (strong and weak points).
  4. Current management plan, to include on-site personnel, operational procedures, rent increase projections, physical improvements, capital, financial needs, etc.
  5. Marketing/leasing plans, including promotional materials, potential tenants, lease considerations and target date for full occupancy.

B. Budget/Finance
  1. Actual operational costs for past year and annualized costs for present year.
  2. Budgets for future operations, including any improvements recommended in management/marketing/leasing plans (detail all assumptions and calculations).

C. Summary and Comparisons of Budgeted Projections

	Prior Year	This Year (Annualized)	Projected Budget
• Rent and other income	$ _____	$ _____	$ _____
• Expenses	_____	_____	_____
• Net operating income	$ _____	$ _____	$ _____
• Operating ratio (expense ÷ rents)	_____	_____	_____
• Vacancy rate (%)	_____	_____	_____

in reading the report. Data collection must come first in order that such conclusions and recommendations can be prepared.

Management Progress Reports

Quarterly financial progress reports should be prepared for the owner(s). Technically, these reports can be prepared from standardized forms (Figure 8.8) that note income and expenses with the aim of understanding any variance from the planned budget.

In practice, these reports must usually be supplemented by written accounts that explain:

Figure 8.7 Market Survey Property Report Outline

I. **Conclusions and Recommendations:**
   A. Conclusions about the market.
   B. Conclusions about the project/property.
   C. Market recommendations.

II. **Market Data:**
   A. Photo and map of area.
   B. Competitive property survey and data.
   C. Miscellaneous information (trends, new laws, etc.).

III. **Project/Property Data:**
   A. Schematic of recent developments close to the property.
   B. Tenant profiles.
   C. Existing/proposed market program.
   D. Existing/proposed rent summary.
   E. Capital needs.

- the reason for variances;
- recent changes in the rental market;
- new construction in the area;
- recently determined physical deficiencies in the property and a plan for corrective action; and
- any other pertinent information that cannot wait for an annual report.

TERMINATING AN ACCOUNT

Adverse conditions noted in the management agreement that arise may warrant cancellation or termination of an account. It is best to handle such situations in the most businesslike manner possible. Initially, this will mean an official written notification of your company's intentions, with a minimum 30-day commencement.

Rather than developing or using a specific termination form, the New Account Takeover Form (Figure 1.2) can be used if reversed where appropriate. Have a sign-off list prepared that shows items being transferred to the new owners/managers. Among other things, this list should include leases, certificates of insurance, rent receipts and rosters, lease assignments, security deposits and the final accounting on all funds.

Figure 8.8   Quarterly Management Progress Report

	ACTUAL	BUDGET	VARIANCE
Property: _____ Date: _____			
Prepared By: _____			
INCOME			
Gross possible income	$ _____	$ _____	$ _____
Less vacancies, allowances	_____	_____	_____
Base rental income	$ _____	$ _____	$ _____
Average occupancy	_____%	_____%	_____%
EXPENSES			
Management fee	$ _____	$ _____	$ _____
On-site management expenses	_____	_____	_____
Advertising and promotion	_____	_____	_____
Grounds and landscaping	_____	_____	_____
Buildings	_____	_____	_____
Utilities	_____	_____	_____
Parking, streets, etc.	_____	_____	_____
Other	_____	_____	_____
TOTAL OPERATING EXPENSES	$ _____	$ _____	$ _____
TOTAL OPERATING INCOME	$ _____	$ _____	$ _____
TOTAL REPAIRS AND REPLACEMENTS	$ _____	$ _____	$ _____
CAPITAL EXPENDITURES	$ _____	$ _____	$ _____
NET BEFORE TAXES, INSURANCE AND DEPRECIATION	$ _____	$ _____	$ _____

TIME UTILIZATION

Whenever we speak of operational efficiency, the key unspoken element is usually *time*. It is unspoken primarily because it is the one aspect of life (business or otherwise) that is totally inflexible. And yet, the business success of property management depends not only upon our level of expertise, but also on the amount of work we can accomplish in a given period of time. Still, while the amount of time available to us cannot be changed, it can be managed if we understand those aspects of life that divert our attention from the job at hand.

The general obstructions to good time use may be divided into seven areas, all of which are unavoidable. They are

- unsolicited telemarketing;
- unnecessary meetings;
- office gossip/politics;
- mixing personal with business relationships;
- socializing;
- interruptions; and
- perfectionism/procrastination.

Acknowledging that these situations will occur is the first step toward controlling them. Interruptions from telemarketers, for example, can be almost completely eliminated by a good secretary or receptionist (or, if you operate a very small business, by a telephone answering machine).

Unnecessary interruptions are probably the biggest time wasters. One manager found an interesting way to cut down on them in the office by posting the time he would be available for interruptions on his door and listing the per-minute cost of non-emergency interruptions for other times.

The other challenges will be more difficult because they are part and parcel of being human. In this respect, pay careful attention to the use of the word *control* rather than *eliminate*. It is doubtful that office socializing, for example, can be completely eliminated nor, in most instances, is it really desirable. An office where people work together but do not really know each other on some personal level is not an office but an assembly line. It is, in fact, impossible to establish any kind of office morale or respect for individuals within the company without some socializing. What's important, therefore, is to encourage the productive aspects of such human activity while discouraging those that are destructive.

In most instances, the misuse of time by managerial personnel will involve

- not delegating work;
- not scheduling work;
- not making decisions;
- not establishing priorities; and
- not communicating.

The misuse of time by non-managerial employees can generally be traced to one of these five areas.

Time Logs

The first part of effective time management is to find out where the time goes. And a good place to start is with your own usage. Researchers at McGill University, for example, studied how effective managers use time. Their conclusion: they don't regularly block out large chunks of time for planning, organizing, directing and controlling. Rather, such time is fragmented, the average interval devoted to any one issue being a mere nine minutes.

Written time logs for all employees are a common method that many service businesses use to keep track of where time goes (and to whom the time should be billed). Figure 8.9 is an example of such a log, although it is best that each property management company design its own. For your company's log to be effective, however, it must be easy to use. The last thing your organization needs is a time log that takes too long to fill out.

For the sake of speed, your log should (1) show 15-minute segments with an entire day on a single sheet and (2) list the most common tasks in a consistent format so that they can be compared to other time sheets. To ensure accuracy, the forms should be filled out, whenever possible, as the day progresses.

How often the logs will be used depends on your needs. Some companies use them daily all year long because they are needed not just for time studies, but for client billing as well. Other companies, particularly small ones where time wastage is readily apparent and difficult to hide, are concerned only with occasional analysis. In this case, quarterly use for stretches of about two to four weeks at a time may suffice.

The time log provides the basis for analyzing the usage of time. Once done, you can identify those practices that seem excessive or unproductive and devise a program to correct the situation.

VISITING THE SITE

At the beginning of this chapter, we noted that the management of properties begins in the company's business office. However, your business won't be able to manage any property effectively from this location unless it is also located at the property site.

Your property management company may have the most efficient employees and a sense of morale second to none, but it will fail if its professional property managers do not visit property sites regularly and often. Only when experienced supervision is readily available on-site will a property management company truly prosper.

Figure 8.9   Daily Time Log

TIME	Client	Account No.	Hours (Quarters)	Code	Description
8:00					
8:15					
8:30					
8:45					
9:00					
9:15					
9:30					
9:45					
10:00					
10:15					
10:30					
10:45					
11:00					
11:15					
11:30					
11:45					
12:00					
12:15					
12:30					
12:45					
1:00					
1:15					
1:30					
1:45					
2:00					
2:15					
2:30					
2:45					
3:00					
3:15					
3:30					
3:45					
4:00					
4:15					
4:30					
4:45					
5:00					
5:15					
5:30					
5:45					
6:00					

NAME: _____ **Date:** _____

CODES:
001 Training   006 Meetings   011 Vacation
002 Recruiting   007 Personal   012 Inspections
003 Supervising   008 Telephone   013 Problem solving
004 Accounting   009 Research   014 Education
005 Budgeting   010 Travel   015 Miscellaneous

Appendix A:
Sample Employee
Information Manual

INTRODUCTION

The Property Management Company is a service business. It serves people both as individuals and as groups. Furthermore, because the company serves people directly, the personal human element is an essential part of the service. Readiness to serve the client or tenant in all respects is as important as your technical knowledge of your work. Accuracy and speed do not count if you cannot be pleasant.

STANDARDS OF ETHICAL CONDUCT

The most important responsibility of a company is to its clients; the officers and the staff are to conduct all of their affairs consistently in a manner that merits trust and confidence. The medium through which a company achieves a reputation for integrity is the collective and individual conduct of its staff. The circumstances of our work require each of us to manage our personal and business affairs so as to avoid a conflict (or even suspicion of a conflict) between our self-interest and our objective job performance. A transaction that *appears* to give rise to a conflict of interest can, under some circumstances, be as embarrassing for the company and the individual involved as a transaction that does in fact give rise to such a conflict.

It is improper to use a company position, directly or indirectly, for private gain, to advance personal interest or to obtain favors or benefits for oneself, a family member or any other person.

The environment in which our business is conducted is constantly changing, and public corporate standards of conduct tend to change with the total society. The public view of a company calls for an ever-vigilant self-examination of our conduct. Numerous situations that we encounter in our work carry the potential for conflict of interest. Primary reliance is placed in such cases upon the individual's own judgment and discretion, but these can best be exercised when there is foreknowledge of pitfalls to avoid.

All members of the staff are expected to give this subject their careful attention and to seek guidance from their supervisors whenever there is any doubt about whether a conflict of interest exists.

CONFIDENTIAL INFORMATION

It is obvious that in the company you have access to many kinds of confidential information about our clients. It is your personal responsibility not to discuss information about or provided by any client; not even with members of your own family. Discussions of these matters within the company should be limited to those necessary for the completion of normal business. *Abuse of customer information will be considered grounds for dismissal without notice.*

FILLING JOB VACANCIES

Vacancies are filled by promotion from within the company whenever possible. If a suitable candidate is not already available on the staff, a new employee will be hired.

Hiring

The policy of the company is to hire the best qualified person for every job, regardless of race, color, creed, national origin or sex. It is, therefore, our policy not only to abide by the letter but also by the spirit of all laws pertaining to fair employment practices.

Offers of employment and starting salary determinations will be made by the personnel officer after consultation with the appropriate department head.

Employment of Relatives

It is the policy of the company not to hire relatives of present officers, employees or directors. Because of this rule, marriage between employees will result in one of the parties leaving our service.

Hiring Former Employees

Employees who have left the company voluntarily and make application for re-employment will be given every consideration. A re-employed person loses all rights accruing from prior service with references to vacations and other benefits.

Hiring of Minors

No minor under the age of sixteen (16) will be employed by the company for any temporary or permanent assignment.

Outside Employment

Staff members are presumed to have elected to make the company their major vocational interest, and for this reason are asked to obtain the approval of the personnel officer before accepting any after-hour position. There is no desire to regulate the time of any staff member beyond regular employment hours. The company must, however, be certain that any outside position by a staff member will in no way conflict with the requirements of his or her duties with the company.

TERMINATION OF EMPLOYMENT

Voluntary

An employee terminating voluntarily is expected to provide adequate notice of such termination, preferably in writing. This notice should be presented to their supervisor two weeks prior to the anticipated date of separation. Terminating employees will be paid for any accrued vacations not yet taken by the date of their leaving. All salary earned will be paid in full on the last day of employment. Terminations resulting from resignations without notice will carry no vacation allowance under any condition.

Involuntary

No Fault of Employee.   Should the company find it necessary to initiate termination of employment, every effort will be made to give advance notice of such action, except in the case of release for cause. In normal involuntary separations occurring through no fault of the employee, separation pay on the following schedule may be provided:

Seniority	Separation Allowance
Under 6 months	None
6 months to 1 year	1 week's salary
1 to 5 years	2 weeks' salary
Over 5 years	Individual consideration

Release for Cause.   Employees released for cause are not eligible for separation allowance. The following reasons, while not complete, are examples of causes for involuntary termination:

- Gross insubordination
- Intoxication
- Drug abuse
- Conviction of civil violation
- Unauthorized absence
- Offensive behavior to a client
- Careless or shoddy work
- Willful violation of company policy
- Theft

No employee discharged for cause will be considered for re-employment. Other reasons for termination will not preclude consideration for re-employment.

DRESS CODE

All employees are expected to be neat and clean and to dress in a manner that will be considered in good taste.

FREQUENCY OF PAY

Payday occurs on the 15th and the last day of the month. If either date should fall on Saturday, Sunday or a holiday, payday will be the last working day prior to the regularly schedule payday.

SALARY ADMINISTRATION

It is the policy of the company to maintain a sound program of salary administration. Through a system of job evaluation and salary surveys, compensation guides that are practical and equitable are developed and maintained for all positions.

All employees and management personnel are considered for salary increases periodically. The frequency of the consideration depends on several factors:

- The position level to which the employee is assigned
- Seniority
- Length of time on present assignment

Any increase that may be awarded must be based on satisfactory job performance and would therefore be considered a merit award.

All employees and management personnel are afforded the opportunity to review their job performance with their supervisor at regular intervals. Performance of all new employees is reviewed 90 days from date of employment and at least annually thereafter.

ATTENDANCE, SICK LEAVE AND ABSENCE POLICIES

Good attendance by the staff is necessary for the company to serve its purpose. Punctuality and attendance records will be given serious consideration with respect to pay increases, promotions and possible terminations. No staff member is expected to work when ill or when a personal emergency makes absence necessary. In case of illness or emergency requiring absence from work, the staff member should notify his or her supervisor before regular reporting time so that adequate preparations can be made to serve our customers properly. Time off from the job may be permitted under special circumstances, either with or without pay depending on the reason for the absence, previous attendance record, seniority or other pertinent consideration.

All absences during the first 90 days of employment will be without pay with the exception of a death in the immediate family.

Personal Illness

After 90 days of service, all full-time staff members are eligible to participate under the company salary continuation program when they are absent because of illness or disability.

The company will allow up to six days' absence per year with pay for nonserious day-to-day illness. In addition to this day-to-day illness allowance, extended leave in cases of serious illness may be granted by the appropriate personnel representative according to the following schedule:

Seniority	Maximum Number of Working Days	
	Full Pay	Half Pay
Under 90 days	0	0
3 months to 1 year	4	4
1–2 years	6	6
2–4 years	10	10
4–6 years	20	20
6–8 years	30	30
8–10 years	40	40
10–12 years	50	50
12–14 years	60	60
14–16 years	70	60
16–18 years	80	50
18–20 years	90	40
20–22 years	100	30
22–24 years	110	20
24–26 years	120	10
Over 26 years	130*	

* 130 working days equals 26 weeks or six months

All cases for which extended leave related to illness is anticipated should be discussed with the employee's supervisor. This schedule of paid absences is available each year and does not have a career cumulative limitation.

Illness in the Family

Absence because of illness in an employee's immediate family will normally be without pay. Exceptions would be permitted during emergency situations. Your supervisor is authorized to approve one day of absence with pay for this reason. Absences with pay in excess of one day must be approved by your supervisor and the personnel officer.

Bereavement Leave

Paid absences because of a death in the immediate family (parents, spouse, brothers and sisters and children) may be approved by your supervisor for up to five days in a local situation and up to seven days in circumstances that would require a considerable amount of travel time. One day with pay may be approved for the death of a grandparent.

Marriage

One day off with pay may be granted by the department supervisor to any employee for the purpose of his or her own marriage.

Birth

One day off with pay may be granted to any male employee when the day is taken in conjunction with the date of birth of his child.

Medical and Dental Appointments

Medical and dental appointments should be scheduled as far as possible in advance with your supervisor. Reasonable time for medical or dental appointments that require only short absences from the company may be allowed at the discretion of your supervisor.

Absence for Reasons Other Than Illness

If an employee wishes to use any of the allotted six days for any purpose other than sickness, it should be done before December 1st of each year. Sick leave days are not accumulative and will not be granted for more than two days in succession. At the end of the year, each employee will be paid one day's pay for each day of sick leave remaining.

Jury Duty

If an employee is called to serve as a juror, this should be viewed as a civic responsibility and necessary time will be granted at full pay. Any fees received as a juror, therefore, are to be turned over to the company, after deducting mileage expense.

Personal Business

Personal business should be scheduled during normal nonworking hours whenever possible. Your supervisor is authorized to approve up to one day of personal time without pay when circumstances warrant. More than one day's leave time must be authorized by the personnel officer.

Maternity Leave

To qualify for maternity leave, an employee must have been employed at least 12 months prior to the birth of the child. Any time over and above sick leave days and vacation earned will be considered the employee's own time and without compensation. The leave will begin at the recommendation of the employee, the employee's physician or the request of management based on employee productivity, safety, attendance or other work-related reasons. In any case, if an employee works beyond the end of the sixth month of pregnancy, written permission will be required from her personal physician. A maternity leave will be granted for a maximum period of 90 days following the birth of the child. The employee may return to work when her physical condition warrants as determined by her personal physician and when a suitable position is available. When the employee returns to work, she will be placed in a job comparable to the position she held prior to leaving at the rate of pay received when the leave commenced, if at all possible. The employee must notify the company in writing 30 days before expiration of the leave, indicating her intention to return or not return to full-time work.

EMPLOYEE BENEFITS

Vacation

The company will provide a suitable annual vacation to all of its permanent employees. The amount of vacation will reflect the employee's length of service and level of responsibility.*

Length of Service	Annual Vacation
0–12 months	0 weeks
1–4 years	2 weeks
5–20 years	3 weeks

* Seniority of service will be the governing factor in the selection of a vacation period.

During each employee seniority year, the employee should be away from his or her job for two consecutive weeks. Since this absence will normally be accomplished through vacation, each employee is expected to schedule his or her vacation so that weeks of vacation will be taken consecutively. Requests for vacation time of less than two consecutive weeks must be approved by the personnel officer, when no other two-week consecutive absence has occurred.

Those eligible for more than two weeks are encouraged to take the additional time in any convenient manner that will not present scheduling problems within the immediate working unit.

If a holiday occurs during an employee's vacation, an additional day off will be granted at a time agreed upon by the individual and the department manager concerned, but preferably the working day before or after the employee's scheduled vacation.

All vacation time will be considered as time worked in computation of overtime pay.

Holidays

One day's pay will be credited to each regularly scheduled full-time employee whose normal work week would have included any company holiday. Days normally recognized as holidays are:

- New Year's Day
- Martin Luther King Day
- Memorial Day
- Independence Day
- Labor Day
- Columbus Day
- Thanksgiving Day
- Christmas Day

Group Life Insurance Plan

The company provides term life insurance policies for all officers and full-time employees. Full details of the plan will be outlined by the personnel officer.

Group Medical Insurance

The company provides a group hospital and major medical plan. Coverage for all full-time employees is provided at no cost. Employees will be charged the extra cost if coverage is extended to include their families.

Education

Because the company encourages self-education and development, it provides financial assistance to all full-time employees who wish to participate in accredited courses. Should you drop out or should you terminate your employment, the company is due a refund of the fees advanced.

Worker's Compensation

The company provides worker's compensation coverage for all employees. Cost of such coverage is paid by the company and covers injuries sustained on the job. If an employee is injured on the job in the course of employment, the employee will be referred to a doctor or emergency hospital. Should the employee have a work injury treated by his or her personal physician, there is a possibility that the insurance company may decline to pay all or part of the charges incurred. Subsequent refusal to submit to an examination by a doctor selected by the insurance company can jeopardize the employee's rights to disability indemnity. A supply of the employer's report form is on hand and forms must be completed by an officer.

Rest Periods

Rest breaks are beneficial to both the employee and the company. For this reason, it is our practice to grant a 15-minute break each morning and afternoon. Although we permit and encourage such breaks, please remember that it is yours and the company's responsibility to take care of our customers without any undue delay. We, therefore, ask that you work with your supervisor in scheduling rest periods.

Overtime

Nonexempt employees are not to work overtime unless they have reached previous authorization from their supervisor. Nonexempt staff members are qualified for overtime payment at the rate of one and one-half times the regular hourly rate for all time worked in excess of 40 hours in any one week.

Employees are classified as exempt or nonexempt in accordance with regulations issued under applicable Federal Wage and Hour Laws. Briefly, an employee whose duties are of an executive, administrative or professional nature is considered an exempt employee. All other employees are classified as nonexempt.

Civic and Professional Memberships

Employees are encouraged to participate in civic and professional organizations. These activities provide opportunities for personal growth, as well as marketing opportunities for the company. The company sponsors many such memberships when approved through appropriate channels.

Reimbursable Business Expenses

It is the policy of the company that no officer or employee should be expected to suffer financial loss because of expenses incurred through travel or company business, promotion of company services, entertainment of customers and prospective customers or participation in approved city or community affairs.

It is expected that we will use both time and money constructively and that entertainment done is appropriate to the business occasion and within the bounds of good judgment.

GENERAL

Personal Financial Affairs

Because of the high degree of trust placed in the company by its clients and the real estate community, it is the policy of the company that every member of the staff shall limit his or her personal phone calls to those that are absolutely necessary and keep them to three minutes or less.

Leaving the Building

Any staff member desiring to leave the building at times other than lunch hours should obtain permission from his or her supervisor, except when engaged in company business.

Telephone Manners

Since a substantial amount of the company's business is conducted by telephone, it is mandatory that a high standard of telephone manners is maintained. Impressions created on the telephone help establish the friendly relationship upon which we depend for continued expansion and growth.

Since efficient telephone service is required throughout each day, good judgment is needed in making or receiving telephone calls. The appropriate way to answer the phone is "Good morning (or good afternoon), Property Management Inc. This is (your name) speaking."

Appendix B:
Sample Accounting
Operations Manual

INTRODUCTION

Whether done by accountants, by computer or by hand, accounting is the process in which records are created, administered and used for historical analysis. This process utilizes various controls on how to handle money when it is received and how to report it. For most, the so-called *cash basis* accounting method (essentially money in, money out) is all that is required. Appropriate forms can be purchased easily or designed to suit.

CASH RECEIPTS

Management Company Cash Receipts

Fees and commissions are usually collected on a monthly basis and should be deposited in the bank daily, as received. All receipts for all accounts will be checked and recorded daily. Dates of deposit must correspond with dates of credit recorded to each project account.

Fees are collected on every property managed by the company. The management fee for each month is usually a percentage of the total income received on each property. This amount will change depending on the income received in a given month. In order to collect all the management fees, the company must make sure that all tenants pay their rent on time.

Management fees are calculated by the 25th of the month. Check requests should be completed and paid no later than the beginning of the following month.

Client Property Cash Receipts

All income is usually collected and deposited in the bank on a daily basis.

Manual Pegboard System

1. All monies must be deposited daily. They cannot be left on the premises overnight.
2. The basic pegboard system consists of three forms: the cash receipt, cash receipt journal and the client ledger card. The cash receipt is used as funds are received. This receipt is placed over the tenant's ledger card, which is then placed over the cash receipt journal, taking care to line up the card receipt with the blank line on the cash receipt journal and card. When the receipt is filled out, it shows the monies received, credits to the proper charges and any balance due. All information is copied through to the ledger card and cash receipt journal for permanent records.
3. A cash receipt journal is to be started at the beginning of each month. During the month, several days' receipts can be recorded on one sheet. There is no need to start a new sheet after each deposit, only at the beginning of each month.
4. All monies, regardless of their source, are to be receipted on the pegboard.
5. Each sheet is totaled and brought forward to the succeeding sheet so that cumulative totals result on the last sheet for the month.
6. Checks received should be endorsed immediately with the "For Deposit Only" stamp. Count and total any cash and checks received and prepare bank deposit slips in triplicate. The total amount on the bank deposit slip must be equal to the total amount on the cash receipt journal for the day.
7. Take all cash and checks to the bank for deposit before the end of the day.
8. Attach each bank receipted deposit slip to its supporting pegboard sheet.

Standard Computer System

1. Endorse all checks with the appropriate "For Deposit Only" stamp immediately upon receipt for deposit.
2. Without exception, balance the day's receipts at the designated time each day.

3. Post the receipts on the ledger cards and in the transaction register to reflect the current balance.
4. Fill out the bank deposit ticket (two copies).
5. The bank deposit amount should total the day's receipts without exception.
6. At designated times during the month, fill out the cash receipt form.
7. When all the cash receipts have been manually recorded on the form, they are ready to be entered into the computer. (Note: Receipts could be entered into the computer on a daily basis.)
   - Get into the main menu of the program and then into cash receipts.
   - Enter Property, Tenant, Amount, Accounts, Total Amount, Deposit Date, Reference and Remarks.
   - Verify each entry. If it is correct, save it and proceed to the next entry.
   - When all the entries have been made, exit to the main menu.

ACCOUNTS PAYABLE

The normal terms on invoices are 30 days from the date of the invoice, unless otherwise stated. All bills must be reviewed as soon as they are received. Accounts payable is divided as follows:

- Incoming bills
- Monthly/yearly payments
- Petty cash
- Cash disbursement

Incoming Bills

1. All incoming bills for the day must be stamped with the date the bills were received.
2. To prevent duplicate payments, payment is made from the invoices only rather than from statements. When reviewing bills, make sure that they are invoices. If the statement is the invoice, it must be so noted. Wherever possible, statements should have invoices as backups.
3. Check for previous balances and then make sure that they have been paid or at least received. If the previous balance has not been paid or received, call the vendor to find an explanation before paying.

4. Fill out check request forms and clip the invoice to the back of the form. Submit check requests for approval
5. Refer to the Charts of Accounts for account numbers.

Monthly/Yearly Payments

1. Refer to the accounts payable listing at the end of each month to prepare check requests for the following month.
2. Annual payments must be approved before checks are written.
3. Due dates on loans are determined by the financing company. These payments should be made before the required dates.

Petty Cash Fund

A petty cash fund is needed to pay small bills such as those for postage, office supplies and similar items. To handle this, a separate account should be set up with reimbursements made based on need. In no case is the balance in this account to drop below 25 percent of its preferred total. For example, if the preferred total is $200, it should not be allowed to drop below $50.

The Petty Cash Recap Report should be used to account for money in this fund.

1. When the office petty cash is down to a predetermined level (say $50), it should be replenished.
2. List each item with the date purchased, description and amount.
3. Count the cash on hand.
4. Total the receipts listed to determine the amount to be replenished.
5. The amount of cash on hand and the reimbursement should equal the total fund that is in the general ledger.
6. Overage should be credited and shortage debited as miscellaneous expense.
7. Assign account numbers to all amounts, but do not use the asset account number for petty cash unless the balance is being increased or decreased. Normally, all charges are to an expense account.

Cash Disbursement

1. Checks are usually written twice a month after bills have been approved.
2. If you are using a computer, follow the process described below:

- Align checks on the printer.
- Get into the main menu of the program and then into Cash Disbursement.
- Enter the Vendor, Amount and Account Number. If there is more than one account, fill in the total amount.
- Do not fill in Date Paid and Reference. The computer will fill them in by itself.
- The description should be entered in the Remarks section.
- After completing each entry, save it and proceed to the next entry.
- When all the Cash Disbursements have been entered, exit to the main menu.
- Select Write Checks, or something similar, from the main menu.
- Enter the Vendor Code. Make sure that the starting check number on the computer is the same as the check that is to be printed.
- Verify each entry.
- Repeat the process until all the checks have been printed.
- Record all the checks on the Check Register after they are printed or print out a computer-generated listing of checks written and enter the total disbursement in the Check Register, referring to the list as back-up data.

PAYROLL

Accurate individual records are kept for each employee showing pay period covered, social security number, address, number of claimed dependents, payroll deductions, date of initial employment and date of termination (if appropriate). Each employee should complete a federal Form W-4. The following steps and procedures will help you to manage payroll and payroll records.

- New Employees—once
- Payroll—twice monthly
- Deposit Tax Requirements for Federal Tax and Social Security Withheld—usually twice monthly, depending on the amount of deposit
- Payment of State Tax Withheld—usually monthly, depending on the amount of deposit
- Deposit of Federal Unemployment Tax—usually quarterly
- Payment of State Unemployment Tax—quarterly (in most states)

- Employer's Quarterly Federal Tax Return—quarterly
- State Quarterly Report of Income Tax Withheld—quarterly
- Form W-2—annually
- Form W-3—annually
- Form 1099s (Miscellaneous)—annually
- Form 1096—annually
- Employer's Annual Federal Unemployment Tax Return—annually
- State Transmittal of Income and Tax Statement—annually

New Employees

1. A new employee should complete an Application for Employment and Form I-9—Employment Eligibility Verification of the U.S. Immigration and Naturalization Service.
2. Have each employee give you a signed Form W-4 by his/her first day of work. This certificate is effective with the first wage payment and will last until the employee files a new certificate. If an employee does not give you a Form W-4, withhold tax as if the employee were a single person who has claimed no withholding allowances. An employee who claims exemption from withholding must renew his/her status by filing a new W-4 by February 15th of each year.
3. Each new employee usually also fills out a State Withholding Form.
4. Set up an individual file for each employee.

Payroll

1. Usually, paychecks are distributed twice a month. The payday for the first 15 days of the month is the 15th and that for the second 15 or 16 days is the last day of that month.
2. Complete the payroll work sheet to determine each employee's net earnings for the pay period. Deduct the following from each employee's pay:
   - The social security tax rate (FICA) for each employee is a percentage of his/her gross salary. The employer has to pay an equal share of FICA.
   - The amount to withhold for federal tax is determined by referring to Circular E, *Employer's Tax Guide* by the Internal Revenue Service.
   - The amount to withhold for state tax is based on each state's laws.

3. When the payroll work sheet has been completed, checks are issued to each employee and distributed on the appropriate dates.
4. Fill out each employee's compensation record every pay period or prepare it through the computer.

Deposit Requirements for Federal Tax and Social Security Withheld

It is important to read federal and state deposit and filing instructions on a regular basis for changes. The following can be used as general rules:

1. Deposit requirements vary depending on the total undeposited taxes. A good rule of thumb is to deposit any undeposited taxes within three (3) banking days after the employees are paid. This practice will avoid late payment penalties, which can accumulate rapidly.
2. Refer to the payroll work sheet to determine the total amount of federal and FICA taxes to be deposited in the bank. Add the totals of the employee's FICA, federal tax withheld and the employer's share of FICA.
3. Issue a check for the total amount payable to your bank. Include the federal identification number on the check.
4. Fill out Form 8109 (Federal Tax Deposit Coupon), indicating the type of tax is 941 and marking the quarter (first, second, third, or fourth) of the year to which the deposit should be applied.
5. Deposit check and Form 8109 on or before the required date at your local bank depository.

Payment of State Tax Withheld

1. State withholdings usually are payable on a monthly basis, and such payments should be postmarked by the 15th day of the month following the month in which the liability was incurred.
2. Refer to the payroll work sheets for the month.
3. Add the total state taxes withheld.
4. Issue a check for the total amount, payable to the state revenue department. Include your state identification number on the check.
5. Complete the state's deposit form, if required.
6. Mail check and form to appropriate department before the 15th day of the following month.

Deposit of Federal Unemployment Tax

1. If, at the end of any calendar quarter, a company owes $100 or more but has not yet deposited the tax, a deposit must be made by the last day of the following month.
2. The Federal Unemployment Tax (FUTA) is .8 percent of the first $7,000 in wages paid to each employee during the year. The tax is imposed on the employer. It must not be collected or deducted from the wages of the employee.
3. Issue a check payable to your bank for the total amount to be paid as FUTA. Include your federal identification number on the check.
4. Complete Form 8109 (Federal Tax Deposit Coupon), Type of Tax 940, and indicate the quarter for which the deposit is being made.
5. Deposit the check and Form 8109 with your bank on or before the required date.

Payment of State Unemployment Tax

1. In most states, the report and amount owed must be mailed to the state before the last day of the month following the end of each quarter.
2. Complete the required form to determine the amount to be paid to the state unemployment department.
3. Issue a check for the total amount, including your state identification number on the check.
4. Send the check and form to the state before the required date.

Employer's Quarterly Federal Tax Return

1. This report, Form 941, is due on the last day of the month following the end of each quarter and is to be mailed to the Internal Revenue Service.
2. Complete the form (Employer's Quarterly Federal Tax Return), showing total withholding and FICA liabilities.
3. Sign and date the return. Mail the report early so that it will reach the IRS before the required date.
4. No payment is necessary unless the amount that is to be deposited in the quarter is insufficient. Depending on the amount of underpayment, it may be necessary to deposit unpaid taxes with a deposit coupon (Form 8109) with your bank instead of mailing them with the return.

State Quarterly Report of Income Tax Withheld

1. This report is usually due on the last day of the month following the end of each quarter and is to be mailed to the state.
2. Complete required forms.
3. Sign, date and mail the report before the required date.
4. Payment may be necessary. Include a check for any undeposited taxes with the return.

Form W-2

1. Copies B, C and 2 of Form W-2 (Wage and Tax Statement) must be given to each employee on the last day of January of the next year. However, if employment ends before the close of the year, the employee may request the form earlier. It must be given to the employee within 30 days of employee's written request if the 30-day period ends before January 31st.
2. Copy D is to be kept in the company's files for at least four (4) years.
3. Copy A should be sent to the Social Security Administration with Form W-3.

Form W-3 (Transmittal of Income and Tax Statement)

A completed Form W-3 is filed with all the Form W-2s sent to the Social Security Administration. The W-3s and W-2s must be submitted by February 28th. Do not staple the W-3s to the W-2s.

Form 1099-Misc. (Statement for Recipients of Miscellaneous Income)

1. Complete a 1099-Misc. form for each contractor who receives $600 or more for service rendered throughout the year.
2. Form 1099-Misc. must be filed with the IRS by February 28th.
3. The recipient should receive a copy of the 1099-Misc. by January 31st.
4. All 1099-Misc. forms must be submitted with a Form 1096.

Form 1096 (Annual Summary & Transmittal of U.S. Information Returns)

1. Form 1096 must be sent with each type of 1099 as the transmittal document. The forms must be grouped by number (i.e., 1099-Misc., 1099-Int.) and each group submitted with a separate Form 1096.

2. Forms 1096 and 1099-Misc. must be submitted to the IRS by February 28th.
3. Mail the report early enough to reach the IRS before the required date.

State Transmittal of Income and Tax Statement

1. This report is filed with the state following the close of the calendar year being reported.
2. The report should be accompanied by all W-2 forms.
3. Do not mail any payment.
4. Check your state's filing instructions for the due date of the report.

Employer's Annual Federal Unemployment Tax Return

1. This report is due at the IRS on the last day of January of the year following the close of the calendar year being reported.
2. Complete Form 940 (Employer's Annual Federal Unemployment Tax Return).
3. Mail the report early so that it reaches the IRS before the required date.
4. No payment is necessary unless the amount deposited for the year is insufficient.

SPECIAL PROCEDURES

Several special procedures need attention throughout the course of business and cannot be neglected. These procedures, which must be carefully evaluated, include:

- Non-Sufficient Funds Check—as required
- Filing Sales Tax—monthly
- Personal Unsecured Property Taxes—annually
- Property Tax Bills—semiannually
- Insurance Billings—annually
- Common Area Maintenance Charges—quarterly
- Missing Money—as required
- Internal Audit—annually
- Monthly Closing Procedure—monthly

Non-Sufficient Funds Check

1. An NSF check returned from the bank is forwarded to the management office.
2. Record the NSF check on the check register and/or ledger card.
3. Hold the NSF check until the account is cleared.
4. Adjust the ledger card to reflect the NSF debit.
5. A collection fee is charged and credited to miscellaneous income.

Filing Sales Tax

1. Application for a sales (rental) tax license follows immediately after a new property has been acquired. Procedures are as follows:
   - Send the completed application and license fees to the state and, if required, to the city.
   - Usually within 14 days, the Sales Tax Return form will arrive. Thereafter this form will be mailed every month to the place of business by the state.
   - The completed sales tax form is usually due by the end of the following month. Check your state and city filing dates.
   - The Sales Tax Return form must be filed monthly even if there is no business activity.
   - Delinquent penalties are usually charged for late payments.
2. Paying sales tax for residential properties involves the following steps:
   - On-site managers will post rents, sales tax, electricity, washer and storage charges they have collected into the cash receipt journal. Copies of the journals are submitted to the office once they are filled.
   - Check to see if the sales taxes collected equal the correct amount and also check for any errors in addition.
   - Check with your state and city for sales tax classifications, rates and codes.
   - Add city tax to all rents collected, if required. However, some states exempt rents for over 30 days from the state tax.
   - Record and enter all receipts into the computer.
3. Paying sales tax for strip shopping centers, office and industrial-commercial properties requires the following procedures:
   - Tenants should mail all rent checks to the office. Record each payment on the tenant ledger cards for each property.
   - Record and enter all receipts into the computer.

Personal Unsecured Property Taxes

Each property should receive a personal property tax form annually from the state taxing authority.

1. These forms must be completed and returned by the date indicated.
2. All purchases for furniture, fixtures and equipment should be placed in a file separate from regular payables.
3. After the form has been completed and mailed, the county will assess the contents and send a billing indicating the amount due.
4. Send payment before the due date.

Property Tax Billings

1. Property tax billings are usually received twice a year. One-half of the taxes are due in the first half of the year and the remainder in the second half of the year.
2. Check the parcel number of the property with the parcel number on the billing to make sure that all billings have been received. The property parcel number list should be updated as changes occur.
3. A valuation notice is received annually from the county for each property. If the tax assessment seems too high, the valuation notice should be given to a company that protests overvaluation immediately so that excessive taxes are not paid. Property owners are given a limited time to file protests.

Insurance Billings

1. The insurance needs of the property should be put out for competitive bid and a company selected based upon the bids received.
2. Insurance premium bills are to be submitted for approval before payment. Compare the billing with the policy to determine that all property is covered.
3. Approval payments are made from funds available. If the required amount is not available, request the necessary funds from the property owners in time for payment on the due date.

Common Area Maintenance (CAM) Charges

1. At the end of every quarter, all CAM charges are billed back to tenants.

2. Tenants are obligated to pay a percentage amount of the costs to maintain the common areas, in accordance with their leases.
3. Each quarter, prepare a spreadsheet indicating all charges paid by the property for the last three months (quarter).
4. After adding the total charges, calculate the percentage due from each tenant based on square footage.
5. Give the spreadsheet to the property manager in charge of the project.
6. Upon approval from the property manager, prepare CAM invoices for each tenant.
7. The CAM invoice will show in detail all charges due from the tenant.
8. Post the charges to the tenant ledger card as a receivable and mail to the tenant.

Missing Money

1. If the amount missing is more than a few dollars, immediately contact the police and have an investigation started.
2. Note the names of officers involved in the original investigation so that you can refer to them later on in the case.
3. Request a copy of the police report.
4. Audit the account to determine the total amount of money missing and the source of the loss.
5. Have all employees fill out sworn statements describing where they were, what they were doing and any facts they know concerning the theft or missing money.
6. Submit a written report with all the above information to the owner.

Internal Audit

1. At least once a year, on an unannounced basis, review each property's on-site bookkeeping system.
2. The main purpose of the review is to make certain that appropriate accounting procedures are being followed. A review should consist of the following steps:
   - Collect a record of transactions received in the office.
   - Trace transactions back through to the tenant ledger cards and bank.
   - Reconcile petty cash.
   - Reconcile daily receipts going to the bank.
   - Check vacancies to see if they might be occupied.

- Check the general appearance of the project.
- Check for possible need for a safe.
- Check vacancies for degree of readiness.
- Confer with managers to help them understand the accounting system.

3. After each review, issue a report of the findings to the property manager and to the owner, noting areas where the accounting procedures are not being followed.
4. Conduct a follow-up review in less than a year if numerous procedures are not being followed.

Monthly Closing Procedures

Procedures to be followed at the end of the month include:

- Balancing accounts
- Reconciliation of bank statements

Balancing Accounts

1. Record all disbursements and receipts on the general ledger.
2. Each property also has its own register. Therefore, when a receipt/disbursement is recorded on the consolidated transaction register, it also has to be entered on the individual property transaction register.
3. At the end of the month, the total amount on the consolidated transaction register must equal the sum of the individual property transaction registers.
4. Verify the ending total of each property on the transaction register with the ending total of the property on the computer.

Reconciliation of Bank Statements   The reconciliation of bank accounts proves the cash balance shown by the general ledger and checkbook and points out any errors made by the bank or by you so that they can be corrected. Most bank statements provide a space for reconciling the account. The reconciliation steps are as follows:

1. List all checks written on or before the last date on the bank statement that were not returned as cancelled checks with the statement.
2. List all deposits made on or before the last date on the bank statement that are not shown on the bank statement.
3. Determine the amount of any bank service charges.

4. To the last balance shown on the bank statement, add the amounts determined by steps 2 and 3 and deduct the amount determined by step 1. The balance should agree with the amount in the checkbook and the general ledger. Prepare any adjusting entries required, including adjusting the book balance for any bank charges.

Chart of Account Codes

ASSETS

1010	Petty Cash
1020	Cash on Hand
1030	Cash in Bank Account #1
1040	Cash in Bank Account #2
1910	Deposits Refundable
2010	Land
2050	Buildings
2060	Paving
2061	Accumulated Depreciation for Paving
2070	Furniture and Fixtures
2071	Accumulated Depreciation for Furniture
2990	Suspense

LIABILITIES

3001	Mortgage Payable
3250	Rental Deposits
3400	Payroll Taxes Payable
3401	FIT Withheld
3402	FICA Withheld
3403	SIT Withheld
3460	Sales Taxes Payable

CAPITAL

4001	Capital #1
4002	Capital #2
4003	Capital #3
4005	Partner Withdrawal #1
4006	Partner Withdrawal #2
4007	Partner Withdrawal #3

INCOME

5001	Rental Income
5002	Guests
5003	Pets
5004	Utilities
5005	Late Charges
5006	Laundry
5007	Pay Phone

Chart of Account Codes (continued)

OPERATING EXPENSES

8002	Office Salaries
8100	Advertising
8130	Accounting and Legal
8180	Bank Service Charges
8210	Collection Fees
8215	Contract Services
8420	Gas, Oil and Tires
8440	Insurance
8445	Insurance—Worker's Compensation
8460	Interest
8550	Management Fees
8580	Miscellaneous
8640	Office Supplies
8660	Outside Services
8700	Park Maintenance
8710	Pest Control
8720	Postage
8750	Repairs and Maintenance
8810	Taxes and Licenses
8820	Taxes—Real Estate
8830	Taxes—Payroll
8840	Taxes—Sales
8870	Travel and Entertainment
8900	Telephone
8920	Utilities
8998	Wages

OTHER INCOME AND EXPENSES

9020	Other Income
9030	Interest Income
9060	Depreciation

Appendix C:
A Property Management
Business Plan Outline

I. Company Description
   A. What kind of business is this?
   B. Describe the service(s) that will be provided, including a comparison with its competition, citing advantages or improvements, if necessary, that would make the company unique.
   C. Why is there a need for this business?
      1. Will it fill an area of specialization not now being handled?
      2. Is the market growing rapidly enough to accommodate a new player?
   D. Describe the potential customers, their characteristics and why they would be inclined to use the company's services.
   E. Explain why the company will do well and any other factors that will lead to success.

II. Company Management and Ownership
   A. Planning
      1. Developing a basic strategy:
         a. How do you plan to achieve business objectives with respect to competition and government regulations?
         b. Prepare a policy statement that clearly informs the reader where the company intends to be five years from now and where it will go from there.
         c. What are the competitive threats over the next five years? Cite examples of successes and failures.
      2. Definition of key operation goals:
         a. Income in dollars.
         b. Profits expected.
         c. Number of properties.

B. Organization
    1. What is the legal form of this business and why was this form selected?
    2. Describe the duties and responsibilities of:
        a. Managers.
        b. Employees.
    3. How many people will be needed and what type(s) of skill(s) will be required?
    4. Prepare an organizational chart to identify key positions and the personnel occupying them.
    5. What are manager's skills and relevant experience? How do they relate to the key success factors for the business (i.e., what are their track records and will they help the business succeed)?
    6. Where does the business intend to attract key people and how will it compensate them? What incentive plans will be used? What will the working conditions be like?
    7. Will there be a Board of Directors? If so, what will be its members' areas of expertise?
    8. In the matter of new employees, will there be an established procedure for:
        a. Selecting and hiring?
        b. Inducting and orienting?
        c. Training and follow-up?
    9. Will there be an established procedure for discipline and/or termination of unsatisfactory employees?
    10. What outside service(s) will be used?
        a. Banker.
        b. Accountant.
        c. Attorney.
        d. Insurance advisor.
        e. Other consultants.
C. Directing
    1. What management and leadership style will be appropriate for the business?
    2. What plans will be put into effect to ensure complete and accurate internal communications?
    3. How will internal problems, complaints and grievances be handled?
    4. How will emergencies be handled?
D. Control
    1. What will be the key indicators of success during normal operations?

2. How will these indicators be monitored?
3. What will be done when unfavorable deviations from the plan are observed?
4. Have budgets been set for:
   a. Expense items?
   b. Revenue expectations?
   c. Profit projections?
5. How will accounts receivable be monitored?
6. What is the basic timetable?
7. What are the control milestones and deadlines?
8. Do you have a backup plan and, if so, what triggers it?

III. Marketing
  A. Market Analysis
     1. Are you in a specialty area of property management?
     2. How big is it now? In five or 10 years?
     3. What are its chief characteristics?
     4. In general, who are or will be your major clients?
     5. What are or will be the major applications of your service? How will they be used?
     6. What are the major trends in the industry that might affect your business?
  B. Target Market
     1. Who are your specific potential customers?
     2. How will you identify them?
     3. What variables will you use to segment your market?
     4. Why do you believe they are valid segmentation variables?
     5. What needs or wants do they have that your service will fill?
     6. How will you communicate with them?
  C. Your Competition
     1. Who are or will be your major competitors?
     2. Why are they successful? What are they doing right?
     3. What is the approximate market share commanded by each of your major competitors?
     4. How important are they in the total market you intend to serve?
     5. Why do you expect your target market to leave your competitors and hire you?
     6. What is or will be the distinctive difference that sets you apart from the competition?

D. Marketing Mix
1. Service
   a. Describe your service in detail.
   b. Describe the history of this service, its position in the industry and any future trends.
   c. For what purpose is your service used?
   d. What are the important features of your service?
   e. Are any of these features proprietary? If so, are they legally protected?
   f. What are the benefits to the customer of your service?
   g. What are your plans for the future development of your service?
2. Price
   a. What is the pricing history of your service?
   b. What are the current pricing trends?
   c. What do you expect for the future?
   d. What is your pricing strategy? Why did you select it?
   e. How do your nearest competitors set price?
   f. What will you do in response to price changes by your competitors?
3. Promotion
   a. What exactly are your advertising plans?
   b. What is your advertising budget?
   c. How did you arrive at it?
   d. What are your plans for generating publicity about your business (as distinct from advertising)?
   e. How will you market your services? Describe your sales force in detail: who will sell, where and their background and training.
   f. Will you use any sales promotion techniques? Describe them, why you selected them and what you expect them to do for your sales.
E. Marketing Environment
1. Describe in detail how any of the following might affect your business or its sales potential:
   a. Legal environment.
   b. Political forces now or in the future.
   c. Regulatory agencies or governmental controls over your industry or firm.
   d. Economic forces.
   e. Social trends.
   f. Technological changes.

IV. Operations
    A. How will you accomplish property management tasks?
        1. How much will you do internally, and how will you do it?
        2. How much will you subcontract out to others?
            a. At start-up and for the first year?
            b. In future years?
    B. What is your present capacity level for office operations?
        1. Is this adequate for near-term needs?
        2. Can this be expanded in the future? How?
        3. Is your facility designed with operations and work-flow efficiency in mind?
    C. What operating advantages do you have? How will you capitalize on them?
    D. Location
        1. Why did or will you locate in the area selected? Are there significant strategic or logistic reasons?
        2. Does your location offer flexibility or opportunity for growth?
        3. Is your location well suited for:
            a. Transportation needs and requirements? Can your employees get to and from work easily? Can your clients find you and get to you easily?
            b. Communication needs?
        4. Have there been any significant recent developments or trends (e.g., population growth, freeways, etc.) that might have an effect in the future on your current choice of location?
    E. Regulations and Laws
        1. What special regulations must be complied with in your specialty (i.e., federal, state and/or local? Licenses, permits, registration, etc.)?
        2. Do you have a recordkeeping and reporting system in place to ensure your compliance and that accurate, timely reports will be filed?
        3. Do any special regulations or agreements govern the use of your chosen business name? If so, what are they and what protections do you have in place?

V. Financing
    A. Present Financial Statements
        1. Balance sheet (current).
        2. Profit and loss statement (Income Statement).

B. Future (Pro Forma) Financial Statements:
1. Year-end balance sheet for the first year of operations.
2. Profit and loss statements by month or by quarter at least until breakeven, then yearly over a five-year period.
    a. Is your breakeven point clearly identified, including the assumptions you used in reaching your conclusion?
3. Other relevant financial planning tools:
    a. Cash budgets.
    b. Monthly cash flow projections.
    c. Capital budgets (i.e., large, important purchases for equipment or other major acquisitions planned).
    d. Have you clearly identified all key assumptions that have been used in your pro formas? Have you stated why you used them instead of alternatives? Did you give your assessment of how reliable or how valid they are likely to be?
C. Sources and Uses of Funds
1. How much money do you or will you need to begin operations?
2. How much money will you need over the next five years if the business succeeds?
3. When exactly will the extra money be used, and what will it be used for?
4. What will be the source of these funds?
    a. Equity sources: Specify how much ownership you and/or others will have in the business.
    b. Debt sources: Specify how much money you will borrow.
        i.   What are the terms for repaying the loan (i.e., interest rate, payback period, other terms)?
        ii. What is the source of the money to meet the repayment schedule?
        iii. What collateral, if any, will you pledge as security?
        iv. What is your back-up plan to repay debts if the business does not work out as you hope?
5. Do you have any plans to go public with a stock offering? If so, what would be the size of the offering, how much capital would you hope to raise and what would be the timing of the offering?

VI. Start-Up Schedule and Timetable
  A. Provide a list of activities, in sequence, that must be accomplished to prepare for the start-up of the business. This should be presented in a fairly detailed document.
  B. Provide a timetable showing when each step is to be completed and the relationships among items that are interdependent. Also list important commitments that must be met.

VII. Critical Risks and Potential
  A. List and discuss the critical risks, problems or other negative factors that might influence the outcome of the plan in the foreseeable future.
    1. Discuss their probability and severity.
    2. What actions and defenses will you take to eliminate or mitigate their effects?

VIII. Appendices or Exhibits
  A. Resumes of your key managers.
  B. Professional references or testimonials. Show your successful relevant track record.
  C. Market studies: Relevant articles from trade journals; contracts or commitments from prospective customers, etc.
  D. Copies of relevant copyrights or other legal protections, documents or certifications that you are required to obtain.
  E. Anything else that you believe is relevant and that would help make your business plan more comprehensive and complete.

Appendix D: Property Management Forms

Commercial Lease Summary

Commercial Lease

Competitive Property Rent Analysis

Complaint/Inquiry—Work Order

Homeowner Violation

Property Inspection Report—Residential

Property Maintenance Assignment and Report

Property Management Agreement

Residential Rental Application Form

Social Activity Checklist

Tenant/Occupancy Profile

Traffic Log

Commercial Lease Summary

Property: _____ Date: _____

Prepared By: _____

Tenant: _____ Unit No.: _____

   Name of Business: _____
   Type of Business: _____
   Home Address: _____
   Work Phone: _____ Home Phone: _____
   Person to Contact: _____

Lease Terms:

   Length of Lease: _____
   Starting Date of Lease: _____
   Ending Date of Lease: _____
   Renewal Option: _____
   Date Option Exercised: _____
   New Termination Date: _____

Rent:

   Monthly Rent: $_____
   Per Sq. Ft. Rate: $_____
   Yearly Rent: $_____
   Rent Increase Date: _____ (Month) _____ (Day) _____ (Year)
   Rent Increase Term: _____
   Last Month Rent: $_____
   Holdover Rent (per month): $_____
   Tax Escalation: _____ Base Yr. (% inc.) _____
   Operation Cost Escalation: _____ Base Yr. (% inc.) _____
   C.P.I. Escalation: _____ Base Yr. (% inc.) _____
   Date First Increase Possible: _____

Others:

   Parking Stalls: _____ @ $ _____/month
   Storage: _____
   Signs: _____
   Insurance Requirements: _____
   Certificate Required: _____
   Special Clauses: _____
   _____

   Remarks: _____
   _____

Instructions:
1. This report is attached to the top of the lease for easy reference.

COMMERCIAL LEASE

DATE:

LESSOR:

LESSEE:

1. *Leased Premises.* Landlord does hereby demise, lease and let unto Tenant the following described areas, rights and privileges (hereinafter collectively referred to as the "Leased Premises"):

   a. The portion of Building which is circumscribed in red on the building floor plan, a copy of which is attached as Exhibit A, consisting of _____ square feet, which portion of the Building is hereinafter referred to as the "Premises":

   b. Such nonexclusive rights-of-way, easements and similar rights with respect to the Buildings and the Premises as may reasonably be necessary for access to, ingress and egress from the Buildings and the Leased Premises; and

   c. The right to use, with all tenants, occupants and users of the Buildings, the restrooms, designated vehicular parking areas and all other common areas of the Property. Tenant is hereby granted the exclusive right to the use of _____ marked parking stalls.

2. *Term of the Lease.* The term of this lease shall be for a period commencing _____, or on the date Tenant opens for business in the Premises, whichever is earlier, and ending on the last day of the ____th complete month following the commencement date.

3. *Rent.* Subject to the provisions of Section 6 below, as base rental for the Leased Premises, Tenant agrees to pay to Landlord the total sum of $_____.

   The monthly base rental for the first year has been computed at a rate of $_____ per square foot per year. The monthly rental rate is $_____ per month ($ _____ × _____ square feet/12 = $ _____) plus applicable sales tax.

   Tenant agrees to pay the rent in manner and form following:

The sum of $ _____ upon the signing of this agreement (the receipt of which is herewith acknowledged by Landlord) as earnest money deposit, to be applied as rent for the first full month and the last full month of this lease;

If the term of this Lease shall commence during a month, the rent for that particular calendar month shall be prorated and computed on the basis of the regular monthly rental rate above set forth and shall be payable forthwith upon the giving of written notice of possession by the Landlord or on the date tenant opens for business in the Premises, whichever is earlier; and,

Thereafter, subject to the provisions of Section 4 below, Tenant shall pay to Landlord as rent for the Leased Premises $ _____ payable on or before the first day of each and every month of the remaining Lease term. Any rents not paid within ten days of the due date are considered delinquent on the eleventh day and subject to a ten percent (10%) late charge.

4. *Increase in Rent.*

    a. Beginning _____ the monthly rental shall be increased 10% to $ _____ plus applicable sales tax.

    b. Beginning _____ the monthly rental shall be increased 10% to $ _____ plus applicable sales tax.

    c. Or Consumer Price Index of the U.S. Average of the Bureau of Statistics, Department of Labor, whichever is less.

5. *Taxes.* In addition to and together with the rents and other charges collected by Lessor, Lessee agrees to pay taxes at the rate of _____ percent per month ($ _____) and any other governmental taxes (except income tax) that may be imposed thereon. Real estate taxes shall be paid by Lessor.

6. *Utilities and Services.* Utilities and services will be supplied by and paid as follows:

	Lessor	Lessee
Gas	_____	_____
Electric	_____	_____
Water	_____	_____
Heating and Refrigeration	_____	_____
Trash Collection	_____	_____
Other	_____	_____
	_____	_____

The Lessor shall not be liable for any delay or failure to apply any of such services due to conditions beyond its control and the Lessor shall not be liable for damage nor shall the Lessee be entitled to any abatement of rent for failure to supply the same.

7. *Signs.* Lessee shall, prior to the commencement date hereof, install, and at all times thereafter maintain, a proper sign or signs on the exterior of the Premises of such size, color, design and location as designated and approved by Lessor. Lessee shall not maintain or display any sign, lettering or lights on the exterior to the Premises unless approved by Lessor in writing. Lessee shall not attach any nonpermanent sign to the inside of any window in the Premises which may be visible through such window from the outside of the building in which the Premises are located, without prior written consent of the Lessor. No rights are granted to Lessee to use the outer walls or the roof of the Premises without Lessor's prior written consent. All lettering on such identification insert panels shall be of such size, color and design as may be approved by the Lessor, and not be in conflict with the rules and regulations of any governmental authority having jurisdiction over such sign. The lettering, maintaining and caring for such insert identification panel, or fractional portion thereof, assigned to Lessee shall be the sole responsibility of Lessee, and shall be accomplished at its sole cost and expense. The lettering shall be accomplished by a company approved by Lessor. Should Lessee fail to pay such company for its services, Lessor has the right, but not the obligation, to pay all costs and expenses incurred by Lessee in connection therewith, and such payment by Lessor shall constitute additional rent payable by Lessee to Lessor on demand. Lessee grants Lessor the right to place "For Lease" and/or "For Sale" signs on the demised Premises thirty (30) days prior to lease termination.

8. *Repairs and Maintenance.* Lessor shall maintain the roof and exterior walls. _____ shall maintain and is responsible for all other repairs/replacements including but not limited to plumbing, toilets, electrical, light fixtures (and all window frames, doors) and ceilings. _____ shall maintain and properly service the heating and cooling units and _____ agrees to pay for replacement of any faulty compressor and motor. Labor for such replacement shall be paid by _____. Any damage to the Premises caused by Lessee including exterior walls, roof and floors occasioned by forcible entry or attempted forcible entry shall be repaired at Lessee's cost.

9. *Lessee's Fixtures.* Any personal property or trade fixtures placed on the Leased Premises by Lessee shall be removed on or before termination of this lease subject to the Landlord's Lien granted herein. Any trade fixtures attached to the Premises shall become the property of Lessor at Lessor's option. Any personal property left in the Leased Premises after possession of the Premises has been returned to Lessor shall be disposed of in any manner Lessor deems best.

10. *Right to Sublease.* Lessee shall not sublet the whole or any part of the Leased Premises, nor assign this Lease without the prior written consent of Lessor, which consent shall not be unreasonably withheld. Any subletting or assignment without the written consent of Lessor shall be voidable at Lessor's option. Lessor's written consent either to an assignment or an entire or partial sublease shall not release Lessee from any obligation under this Lease.

11. *Right of Inspection and Repair.* In the event Lessee fails to make necessary repairs to the Premises after receiving ten days' written notice from Lessor, Lessor may then enter and make such necessary repairs and Lessee agrees to pay for the same. Lessor is granted right of interior inspection during reasonable business hours.

12. *Personal Injury Damage Liability.* Lessor shall not be liable to any person or property for damages sustained as a result of the condition of the Leased Premises unless Lessor has failed to make proper repairs after reasonable written notice thereof. This provision shall especially apply to any type of water damage.

13. *Insurance.* Landlord shall secure, pay for and at all times during the term hereof maintain insurance providing coverage upon the Buildings and Leased Premises, except as noted otherwise, in an amount equal to the full insurable value thereof (as determined by Landlord) and insuring against the perils of fire, extended coverage, vandalism and malicious mischief. All insurance required hereunder shall be written by reputable, responsible companies licensed in the State of _____ .

    Tenant shall, at all times during the term of this Lease, and at its own cost and expense, procure and continue in force the following coverage:

    a. Bodily Injury and Property Damage Liability Insurance with a combined single limit for bodily injury and property damage of not less than _____ ($ _____) Dollars.

b. Fire and Extended Coverage insurance, including vandalism and malicious mischief coverage, in an amount equal to the full replacement value of all fixtures, furniture and improvements installed by or at the expense of Tenant.

Such insurance may, at Tenant's election, be carried under any general blanket coverage of Tenant. A renewal policy shall be procured not less than thirty (30) days prior to the expiration of any policy. Each original policy or a certified copy thereof, or a satisfactory certificate of the insurer evidencing insurance carried with proof of payment of the premium shall be deposited with Landlord within thirty (30) days of commencement date of the term hereof and such anniversary date thereafter.

Landlord and Tenant each hereby waive any and all rights of recovery against the other or against the officers, employees, agents and representatives of the other, on account of loss or damage occasioned to such waiving party or its property or the property of others under its control to the extent that such loss or damage is insured against under any Fire and Extended Coverage insurance policy which either may have in force at the time of such loss or damage. Tenant shall, upon obtaining the policies of insurance required under this Lease, give notice to the insurance carrier or carriers that the foregoing mutual waiver of subrogation is contained in this Lease.

14. *Fire Damage or Other Casualty.* Should the Leased Premises be partially damaged or totally destroyed by fire or other catastrophe not caused by Lessee's negligence, this Lease may be terminated by either party provided the Premises cannot be reasonably restored within ninety (90) days. In the event of such termination the rent shall be prorated to the date said Lease is terminated provided proper written notice is given. Lessor shall not be liable to Lessee for any loss of business or other damage as a result of such destruction.

15. *Notices.* Any notice to be given by Lessor to Lessee shall be sent to the Leased Premises or _____

_____.

Any notices to Lessor from Lessee shall be mailed to _____

_____

or such other place as may be designated from time to time by Lessor. All notices shall be given by depositing same in the U.S. mails, properly addressed with postage prepaid for delivery by Certified Mail with return receipt requested and notices shall be considered as given at the time received by the addressee or personally delivered to the above addresses.

16. *Prior Termination*. Should Lessee fail to pay any rent when due, or should Lessee breach any other condition of this Lease and fail to cure such other default within ten (10) days after notice is given by Lessor, then Lessor may terminate the Lease without further notice and re-enter and rent the premises on whatever terms are reasonable in order to mitigate Lessor's damages. Lessor, in the event Lessee files, or if there shall be filed against Lessee, any petition for bankruptcy or receivership, this lease may be terminated at Lessor's option.

17. *Condemnation*. It is agreed between the parties thereto that if the whole or any part of said Premises is taken by a competent governmental authority for any public or quasi-public use or purpose, then and in that event this Lease shall cease and terminate as of the date when possession of the part so taken shall be required for such use or purpose. All damages awarded for such taking shall belong to Lessor. Lessee shall not be entitled to any compensation obtained by Lessor.

18. *Landlord's and Mechanic's Liens*. Lessor shall have a first lien for the payment of the reserved rent and any other sums due hereunder on all personal property owned by Lessee which may now be or which may hereafter be placed in or on the Leased Premises. Lessee shall pay all liens of contractors, subcontractors, mechanics, laborers and materialmen, and will idemnify Lessor against all costs and attorneys' fees incurred in the defense of any suit in discharging said premises from any liens, judgments or encumbrances caused by Lessee. Furthermore, Lessee shall not have any authority to create any liens for labor or materialmen on the Lessor's interest in the Leased Premises.

19. *Alterations and Improvements*. No alterations shall be made or caused to be made by Lessee to the Leased Premises without Lessor's prior written consent. Any authorized alterations or improvements to the demised Premises shall become the property of Lessor at Lessor's option. This shall include but not be limited to installation of heating, air conditioning, carpeting, partitions and lighting.

20. Holdover Tenancy. In the event Lessee remains in possession of the demised premises after termination of this lease without renewal of this lease, Lessee shall become a tenant on a hold-over month-to-month basis. Monthly rent shall be automatically increased ten percent (10%). All other conditions of this Lease shall apply and either

Party may then terminate the rental by giving thirty (30) days' prior written notice.

21. *Attorneys' Fees and Other Costs.* In the event any legal proceedings arise out of this agreement, the prevailing party shall be entitled to attorneys' fees and costs as determined by the court and not a jury. In the event Lessor exercises the Landlord's Lien granted herein and locks out the Tenant for failure to pay rents, then Lessee agrees to pay Lessor or Lessor's agent said cost to be not less than $25 for expenses incurred in such event.

22. *Waiver.* A waiver of any condition or covenant in this Lease by either party shall not be deemed to imply or constitute a further waiver of any other or like condition or covenant herein.

23. *Legal Responsibility.* This Lease shall apply to and be binding upon the successors, heirs and assigns of the parties hereto and any mention of the singular shall include the plural and of the plural, the singular.

SPECIAL PROVISIONS:

IN WITNESS WHEREOF, the parties have executed this Lease as of the day and year first above written.

TENANT:

By: _____ Date _____

LANDLORD:

By: _____ Date _____

Competitive Property Rent Analysis

For City/Property Areas: _____   Date: _____   Prepared By: _____

PROPERTY NAME/ADDRESS	AGE OF PROPERTY	UNITS/SQ. FT.	TYPE OF RESIDENTIAL PROPERTY*	RENT RANGE	UTILITIES INCLUDED **	DATE OF LAST RENT INCREASE (IF APPLICABLE)	AMENITIES		RATING ***	SPECIAL SERVICES	COMMENTS
							MOST OUTSTANDING	OTHER THAN AVERAGE			

*   Type of Property: A—Adult, F—Family, C—Combination.
**   Utilities Included In Rent: Y—Yes, N—No.
*** Rating: 1—Lowest, 5—Highest.

Instructions:
1. This report should be completed at least once a year.
2. A copy to be sent to the home office with any pictures, brochures, news articles or personal comments, occupancy marketing progress and other information.

Complaint/Inquiry—Work Order

Property: _____ Date: _____

Prepared By: _____

Tenant: _____ Phone Number: _____

Address/Unit: _____

_____

Complaint/Inquiry: _____

_____

_____

_____

_____

_____

_____

_____

_____

_____

_____

_____

_____

Action/Work Order: _____

_____

_____

_____

_____

_____

_____

_____

_____

_____

_____

_____

_____

_____

By: _____ Date Completed: _____

Reviewed By: _____ Date: _____

Instructions: File by unit number when completed.

Homeowner Violation

Property: _____   Date: _____

Prepared By: _____

A number of violations regarding the governing of the legals—C.C. & R's and Bylaws—and also of the Rules and Regulations of the association have been observed in and around the complex. Your assistance is requested in making the complex a better place in which to live.

The following violations have been observed concerning your unit:

1. _____
   _____
   _____
   _____

2. _____
   _____
   _____
   _____

3. _____
   _____
   _____
   _____

4. _____
   _____
   _____
   _____

5. _____
   _____
   _____
   _____

It is requested that the above change(s) and/or correction(s) be completed by _____. If the above are not completed by the date shown, the only alternative the association and management have is to complete and charge to you for the completion. A minimum of $_____ will be imposed for any work that is completed at your unit plus material and labor costs.

If you have any questions regarding the above, please contact this office.

Instructions:
1. This report should be completed on an as-needed basis.
2. Keep a copy for the files.

Property Inspection Report—Residential

Property: _____   Date: _____

Prepared By: _____

	O.K.	NOT O.K.	N/A
GROUNDS			
Block walls—Fence			
Entrances			
Gutter, drains and roods			
Landscaping			
Mailboxes			
Parking bumpers/secured			
Parking lots/without hazard			
Patios/carports/balconies			
Playground/without hazard			
Roadway/without hazard			
Sidewalk street lighting			
Signs			
Speed bumps/painted			
Sprinklers/not creating hazard			
Storage			
Trash enclosure			
Utility systems			
Walkway and steps/without hazard			
AMENITIES			
Barbeque			
Billard rooms			
Exercise equipment/without hazard			
Laundry equipment/without hazard			
Others			
Sauna bath/shut-off switch			
Shuffle board			
Swimming pool area:			
• Depth easily visible			
• Fenced or enclosed			
• Furniture/free of defects			

Property Inspection Report—Residential (continued)

	O.K.	NOT O.K.	N/A
• Gate—self-locking			
• Jacuzzi			
• Non-skid paint			
• Pool rules signs posted			
• Safety equipment available			
BUILDING			
Air conditioning/heating/hot water			
Carpet and drapes			
Electric appliances			
Elevators			
Emergency lighting			
Exercise equipment/without hazards			
Fire equipment available/working			
Floors treated with non-slip wax			
Furnace filters changed regularly			
Kitchen equipment/without hazards			
Library			
Paint			
Restrooms			
Stage/without hazards			
Vending machines/without hazards			
UNITS			
Air conditioning/heating			
Appliances/working			
Carpets/drapes			
Fire equipment			
Furniture			
Hot water heater			
Storage			
Unauthorized items—clutter			
Utility connections safe and working			
Vacant units clean			

Property Inspection Report—Residential (continued)

Other hazards/comments:

_____

_____

_____

_____

_____

_____

_____

_____

_____

_____

Instructions:
1. This report is due on an as-needed basis.
2. All "NOT O.K." checks require a written response or footnote.
3. Where items contain a slash "/", this means there are two questions, i.e., parking lots are clean and proper plus there are no tripping hazards.
4. Keep one copy for on-site files.

Property Maintenance Assignment and Report

Property: _____   Date: _____

Prepared By: _____

	FREQUENCY*	INITIAL	COMMENTS
GROUNDS			
Empty trash/garbage cans	D		
Pull weeds	D		
Water lawns/landscaping (summer)	D		
Fertilize lawns/ground covers	T		
Mow lawns	W		
Sharpen lawn mower blades	T		
Prune trees/shrubbery	T		
Clean/Adjust drinking fountain	D		
Clean car wash	D		
Clean car wash sump	M		
Sweep sidewalks/streets	W		
Clean gutters/downspouts	S		
Check sewer lift pump	W		
Inspect septic tanks	S		
Reset timer-controlled lights	S		
Reset automatic sprinkler system	S		
AMENITIES			
Test pool	D		
Clean/Vacuum pool	D		
Clean pool tile	W		
Backwash pool filter	W		
Inspect pool heater	M		
Clean laundry room	W		
Clean shuffleboard courts	W		
Wax shuffleboard courts	S		

Property Maintenance Assignment and Report (continued)

	FREQUENCY*	INITIAL	COMMENTS
BUILDING			
Clean restrooms	D		
Vacuum/Sweep floors (rec. hall)	D		
Mop floors (rec. hall)	W		
Clean grease trap (rec. kitchen)	W		
Clean/Wax floors (rec. hall)	T		
Wash walls inside rec. hall	T		
Wash windows in rec. hall	T		
Inspect roofs of rec. hall	S		
Repair damaged flashing around roof vents	T		
Clean/Clear wash basin traps	T		
Clean heater and a/c filters	M		
Oil/Lubricate heater and a/c	T		
Replace fans/belts in electric motors as needed	T		
Drain water heater according to manufacturer's instructions	T		
Check water heater pressure	W		

*D—Daily, W—Weekly, T—Two to six months, M—Monthly, S—Seasonal

Instructions:
1. This report is due monthly.
2. Report any potential problems or losses to manager.
3. Keep a copy in the files.
4. Maintain a checklist of facilities and equipment, including recreational equipment, to make sure that everything is covered each day.

PROPERTY MANAGEMENT AGREEMENT

THIS AGREEMENT, made and entered into this the _____ day of
_____ . 19 ____ , by and between _____
(hereinafter referred to as "Owner"), and _____
(hereinafter referred to as "Agent").

In consideration of the property management services to be rendered
by Agent pursuant to this Property Management Agreement, the Owner
hereby designates Agent as the "Exclusive Agent" and representative of
Owner for the purposes of management and operation for Owner's account
of the following described Property: _____
_____
_____
_____
_____

(hereinafter referred to as "Property").

Agent and Owner agree that their respective authorities, duties and responsibilities with respect to the Property shall be as follows:

I. DUTIES OF AGENT

    A. The Agent shall use all reasonable efforts to lease available
space in the above described Property to desirable tenants.
For this purpose, the Agent may employ the services of real
estate brokers. In order to promote such leasing, the Agent
may place newspaper advertising, post "renting" signs,
prepare circulars and engage in other forms of advertising,
subject to the approval of the Owner, at the Owner's expense. The Owner shall refer all inquiries for Leases or Renewal of Leases to the Agent, and all negotiations for
Leases and Renewals shall be conducted or controlled by
the Agent.

    B. Agent shall take all reasonable and necessary action to col-
lect rentals, charges or other income when due from tenants of said property in accordance with the terms of their
tenancies and may execute all receipts or other documents
reflecting receipt of said sums on behalf of the Owner.

    C. All sums received from rents, sales of gas, electricity, sup-
plies and services and other income from the Property shall
be deposited in a "trust account" maintained by the Agent.
The Agent may withdraw from such bank account all dis-

bursements which under this Agreement are to be made at the expense of the Owner. Employees of the Agent who are responsible for monies of the Owner shall be bonded by a Fidelity Bond. The Agent shall render to the Owner a monthly statement of receipts and disbursements, and shall from time to time pay to the Owner all amounts in said account, except a reasonable balance for working cash.

D. From gross revenues collected from the Property, Agent shall:

1. Pay all operating expenses incurred through renting, servicing, maintaining or repairing the Property and such other expenses in connection with the Property as may be authorized by Owner.

2. Pay such sums to lenders as may be designated in writing by Owner on loans secured by or otherwise affecting the Property. Debt service paid by _____, including taxes and insurance.

3. Pay real and personal property taxes and other taxes or assessments levied and assessed against the Property to the extent required pursuant to the procedure which Owner shall select and initial below. _____

   a) Agent shall establish a Revenue Reserve by withholding from gross the estimated annual taxes, and then pay such taxes from this Reserve Account prior to delinquency. _____

   b) Agent shall pay such taxes, provided that Owner shall make funds available to Agent to pay each installment thereof promptly upon notice from the Agent, given at least fifteen (15) days prior to the date of delinquency of such taxes. _____

   c) Owner shall pay all such taxes and Agent shall have no responsibility for payment of same.

E. Agent shall do everything reasonably necessary for the proper management of the Property, including, without limitation thereto, periodic inspections, handling all tenant requests and negotiations, supervision of maintenance and arranging for such improvements, alterations and repairs as may be required of Owner. Agent shall purchase all

materials and supplies, contract with independent contractors
to supply services, make contracts for electricity, gas, window cleaning, refuse disposal, vermin extermination and
for any other utilities or services which the Agent shall reasonably consider as advisable, and shall expend such sums
as Agent deems necessary to accomplish the foregoing.
Agent shall obtain approval from Owner for any expenditure for repairs, improvements or work in excess of
$ _____ for any one item, except monthly or recurring operating charges and/or emergency repairs in excess
of the maximum, if in the opinion of Agent such repairs
are necessary to prevent additional damage or a greater total expenditure or to protect the Property from damage or
to maintain services or conditions to the tenants as called
for by their tenancy. The Agent shall notify the Owner
promptly whenever emergency repairs have been ordered.

F.   The Agent shall employ, discharge, supervise and pay, on
behalf of the Owner, all servants, employees or contractors
considered by the Agent as necessary for the efficient management of the building.

G.   Agent may contract on behalf of the Owner for the sale of
drinking water, paper, gas, electric current, repair service,
towel supplies and other miscellaneous supplies. The income from such contracts shall be the property of the
Owner and shall be deposited by the Agent in the Owner's
account.

H.   Agent shall have the authority and exclusive right to negotiate leases and month-to-month tenancies with existing
and prospective tenants upon terms and conditions approved by Owner.

I.   Agent shall maintain full and accurate books and records
of the accounts of the property, which shall be open to the
inspection of Owner at the office of Agent after reasonable
notice to Agent. Agent shall render to Owner a monthly
statement showing all receipts and disbursements, together
with supporting vouchers, if requested, and reflecting the
financial condition of the Property for the month immediately preceding. At such time, unless otherwise instructed,
Agent shall forward to the Owner the balance remaining
after all necessary charges have been made as provided in
this Agreement. Said monthly statement shall be deemed

accurate and correct between the parties unless Owner notifies Agent within thirty (30) days after the date of said statement of any claimed error or inaccuracy. In the event there is a deficit in the account of the Property, Agent shall notify Owner of the amount of this deficiency, and Owner agrees to forward this amount to Agent within twenty-four (24) hours after notice.

II. DUTIES OF OWNER

A. Owner agrees to promptly furnish Agent with all documents and records to properly manage the Property, including, but not limited to, leases and the amendments and correspondence pertaining thereto, reports on the status of rental payments and copies of existing service contracts.

B. Except for Agent's willful misconduct, Owner shall indemnify and save the Agent harmless from any and all costs, expenses, attorneys' fees, suits, liabilities, damages from or connected with the management of the property by Agent or the performance or exercise of any of the duties, obligations, powers or authorities herein or hereafter granted to Agent.

C. Owner hereby waives all of its rights and those of its insurers with respect to recovery against the Agent and the officers, employees and representatives of Agent on account of loss or damage to Owner's real or personal property where such loss is caused by an insurable peril, including but not limited to fire or any of the extended coverage hazards and which damages arise out of or in connection with the premises. Owner shall give notice to the insurance carrier, if any, that the foregoing waiver of subrogation is contained in this Agreement.

D. In the event that any government agency, authority or department shall order the repair, alteration or removal of any structure or matter on the Property, and if after written notice of the same to the Owner by such body or Agent, the Owner fails to authorize the Agent, or others, to make such repairs, alterations or removal, the Agent shall be released from any responsibility in connection therewith, and Owner shall be answerable to such body for any and all penalties and fines whatsoever imposed because of such failure on Owner's part.

E. Owner shall pay Agent for its leasing services that sum of monies equal to _____ percent of total rents for the total lease period to be payable from first month's rent. Also Agent is authorized to deduct a _____ percent monthly management fee (amount to be determined based on monthly rent) for said services each month as the first charge upon all gross monthly income received for such month. Gross monthly income includes, without limitation thereto, rents, tax clause payments, washer and dryer income, advance or prepaid rent payments when received and all sums collected from the Property, but excludes capital contributions by Owner, refunds and insurance settlements.

III. MISCELLANEOUS

A. This Agreement shall become effective as of the _____ day of _____ 19 ____, and shall continue in full force and effect for a period of twelve (12) months from the effective date, subject to either party's right to cancel this Agreement by not less than _____ (   ) days' advance written notice at any time during said period. At the expiration of the twelve (12) month period, if this Agreement has not been renewed by both parties in writing for an additional fixed period, it shall be deemed a month-to-month agreement, cancellable by either party on not less than thirty (30) days' advance written notice, which notice may be given at any time during the month provided that in any event the cancellation shall be effective at the end of the calendar month during which the thirty (30) day notice period expires.

B. Agent shall, provided Owner has paid to Agent all sums due Agent under this Agreement, deliver to Owner within thirty (30) days after the expiration or termination of this Agreement, the following:

1. An up-to-date accounting reflecting the balance of income and expenses on the property as of the date of the termination.

2. Any balance of monies of Owner held by Agent.

3. All leases, receipts for deposits, insurance policies and unpaid bills which are the property of Owner.

After the delivery of the above designated items to Owner, if Owner does not notify Agent in writing within fifteen (15) days specifying any claimed inaccuracy in said accounting in the amount of monies delivered or in the papers and documents of Owner, or of any claims of Owner against Agent, the Agent shall be deemed to have delivered all monies and documents to Owner and Agent shall be released by Owner from any and all liability or obligation to Owner arising out of this Agreement and the performance thereof by Agent.

C.   Where legal assistance is required for such matters as enforcing the collection of rents or eviction proceedings, such action shall be through Counsel designated by Owner and shall be at Owner's expense. In the event Agent or Owner shall institute legal proceedings against the other, arising out of the terms of this Agreement, or the performance thereunder, then the prevailing party shall recover from the other, all attorneys' fees, costs and expenses incurred in any such action.

D.   This Agreement shall be binding upon the parties hereto, their legal representatives, successsors and permitted assigns, and may not be assigned by the Agent without the prior written consent of the Owner.

IN WITNESS WHEREOF, the parties have executed this Agreement the day and year above set forth.

_____   _____

By _____   By _____

Its _____   Its _____

_____   _____
(Street Address)   (Street Address)

_____   _____
(City, State, Zip)   (City, State, Zip)

_____   _____
(Business Telephone Number)   (Business Telephone Number)

"AGENT"   "OWNER"

Residential Rental Application Form

Property: _____ **Date:** _____

Prepared By: _____

General:

  Name of Applicant: _____

  Home Phone No.: _____

  Indicate Number of Persons Desiring To Occupy _____ Apartment

  Or _____ Mobile Home Space

Name	*Relationship*	*Social Security No.*	*Driver's License No.*	*Age*

Nearest Living Relative: (Other Than Co-Resident)

  Name: _____ Relation to Applicant: _____

  Address: _____

  Phone No.: _____

Present and Past Housing Records:

  Present Address: _____

  Length of Stay: _____ Rent Amount: _____

  Name and Phone No. of Owner/Agent: _____

  Past Address: _____

  Length of Stay: _____ Rent Amount: _____

  Name and Phone No. of Owner/Agent: _____

Employment History:

  Name of Current Employer: _____

  Address: _____

  Phone No.: _____ Occupation: _____

  Income: _____ No. of Years On Job: _____

Financial Information:

  Bank: _____ Branch: _____

  Checking Account No.: _____

  Savings Account No.: _____

  Other Accounts _____

Residential Rental Application Form (continued)

Pets:

If You Have Dogs, Cats or Other Pets, Please Provide Following Information:

Name	*Age*	*Type*	*Color/Description*	*Size*

Automobile Information

Make of Automobile: _____

Model: _____ Year: _____

License Plate No.: _____

Registered Owner: _____ Phone No.: _____

Address: _____

Mobile Home Information (Mobile Home Parks Only):

Serial No.: _____ License No.: _____ Size: _____

Legal Owner: _____ Phone No.: _____

Address: _____

Registered Owner: _____ Phone No.: _____

Address: _____

Reference:

Business: Name: _____

City: _____ Phone No.: _____

Business: Name: _____

City: _____ Phone No.: _____

Personal: Name: _____

City: _____ Phone No.: _____

Personal: Name: _____

City: _____ Phone No.: _____

I authorize the companies, agencies and persons named above to provide information to the property manager regarding character and financial references as prospective tenants.

Signature: _____

Signature: _____

Date: _____

Social Activity Checklist

Property: _____   Date: _____

Prepared By: _____

	IN PLACE	NOT POSSIBLE	COMMENTS
GAMES			
Bridge			
Canasta			
Cribbage			
Pinochle			
TRIPS			
Bus tours			
Tag-A-Long (field trips)			
FOOD-RELATED ACTIVITIES			
Barbecues			
Biscuit and gravy			
Chili			
Cookout			
Holiday dinner—Christmas			
Holiday dinner—Easter			
Holiday dinner—Mother's Day			
Holiday dinner—St. Pat's Day			
Holiday dinner—Thanksgiving			
Koffee Klatch			
Pancakes			
Potluck			
Spaghetti			
Tea			
50th Anniversary			
LESSONS PROVIDED			
Dancing			
Hobbies			

Social Activity Checklist (continued)

	IN PLACE	NOT POSSIBLE	COMMENTS
Painting			
Sewing			
Swimming			
EXERCISE RELATED			
Aerobics			
Bike riding			
Swimming			
Walking			
Yoga			
OTHER ACTIVITIES			
Art shows			
Ballroom dancing			
Billiards			
Bingo			
Church services			
Films			
Golf			
Horse shoe			
Hymn singing			
New Year's Eve			
Outside speaker/entertainment			
Parades—Pets/St. Pat's Day			
Shuffleboard			
Square dancing			
Rock hounds (Lapidary)			

Instructions:
1. Review social activities at least once a year.
2. Add or subtract activities from this list based on needs, interest or facilities available.
3. Each year an effort should be made to help create interesting activities that tenants can enjoy and run themselves. Observe other successful properties.

Tenant/Occupancy Profile

Property: _____   Date: _____   Prepared By: _____

UNIT NO.	TENANT NAME	AGE(S)	MARITAL STATUS !	RETIRED	ONE OR BOTH* WORK	OCCUPATION**	PLACE OF OCCUPATION AREA/CITY	REFERRAL	PREVIOUS YEARS***	REASON CHOSE PROPERTY !!	DATE RSVR	DATE MOVE IN	COMMENTS
GENERAL INFORMATION		HOUSEHOLD			OCCUPATION			RESIDENCY			OCCUPANCY		

! C—Couple, SM—Single men, SW—Single women, K—Children.
!! CH—Clubhouse, P—Pools, SB—Shuffleboard, S—Sauna, L—Location, SA—Social Activities, O—Others.
* O—One, B—Both.
** M—Manager, C—Clerical, S—Services, P—Professional, T—Technical, M/T—Maintenance & Production, O—Others.
*** H—House, C—Condo, A—Apartment, MH—Mobile Home.

Instructions:
1. This report should be completed on an as-needed basis.
2. Send a copy to the home office.

Traffic Log

Property: _____   Date: _____   Prepared By: _____

DATE	PROSPECT'S NAME/ADDRESS	PHONE NO.	AD MEDIA*	UNIT/SQ. FT. NEEDED	DATE NEEDED	QUALIFIED Y/N	DEP. Y/N	COMMENTS**	FOLLOW UP

* Advertising Media: 1. Newspaper—Which? 2. Yellow Pages 3. Sign 4. Drive by—When?
    5. Unit Referral—(a) agency—which? (b) tenant—who? (c) other—specify.

** Comments: Specify why prospect did not rent 1. unit not available 2. too small 3. too expensive 4. inadequate facilities
    5. possible future tenant 6. put on waiting list 7. other—specify

Instructions:
1. This report is due on an as-needed basis.
2. Mail copy to the home office.
3. Follow up on each prospect.

Appendix E: Office Management Forms

CAM Charges Spreadsheet

Check Request

Delinquency Report—Commercial

Delinquency Report—Residential

Expense Report

Individual Time Record

Marketing Checklist

Occupancy Report

Petty Cash Recap

Tenant Roster—Commercial

Tenant Roster—Residential

Tool and Equipment Inventory

Utility Log

CAM Charges Spreadsheet

Property: _____   Date: _____

Prepared By: _____

	TRASH	WATER	ELECTRIC	SEWER REPAIRS	SWEEPING/ CLEANING	ELECTRIC REPAIRS	OTHERS	TOTAL
Jan.								
Feb.								
Mar.								
1st Qtr.								
Apr.								
May								
Jun.								
2nd Qtr.								
July								
Aug.								
Sep.								
3rd Qtr.								
Oct.								
Nov.								
Dec.								
4th Qtr.								
TOTAL								

Instructions:

1. To be filled in on a monthly basis. At the end of each quarter, tenants will be billed accordingly.

Check Request

Property: _____   Date: _____

Prepared By: _____

Check Number: _____   Date of Request: _____

Due Date: _____   Date Check Required: _____

Vendor I.D.: _____

Account Number: _____

Amount Due: _____

Invoice/Description: _____

_____

_____

_____

_____

_____

Disposition Of Check By Accounting:

_____ Return to person requesting check   _____ Mail to payee

_____ Payee will pick up   _____ Other

Check Requested By: _____

Authorized Signature: _____

Instructions: Complete accordingly. Back up with invoice or statement.

Delinquency Report — Commercial

Property: _____   Date: _____   Prepared By: _____

ADDRESS/SUITE(S) NO.	TENANT NAME	TOTAL DUE	BASE RENT	SALES TAX	MISC.	CURRENT MONTH	RENTS			BALANCE DUE	COMMENTS
							30 DAYS	60 DAYS	90 DAYS		

Instructions:

1. This report is to be sent to the home office on the 10th of each month.
2. If no delinquencies occurred during the month, write "no delinquencies" on the report and forward.
3. The income for the month for each property plus any delinquencies will equal the total monthly scheduled rents.
4. Under no circumstances will a delinquency be allowed for over 30 days. If tenant is over 30 days late, an eviction notice should be sent by certified mail with receipt requested to show proof of mailing. If the rent is over 15 days late, send out a seven-day notice to comply.
5. Any common area maintenance charges, percentage rents or other charges are to be added to the miscellaneous column and explained in the comments column or on a separate sheet of paper.

Delinquency Report — Residential

Property: _____   Date: _____   Prepared By: _____

UNIT NO.	TENANT NAME	TOTAL DUE	AGED		NOTICE SERVED	SENT TO ATTORNEY	ACTION TAKEN (date accomplished)				
			CURRENT MONTH	30 DAYS OR MORE			ACTION TAKEN	DATE SERVED	TRIAL DATE	EVICTION DATE	MOVE OUT

Instructions:
1. This report is to be sent to the home office on the 10th of each month.
2. If no delinquencies occurred during the month, write "no delinquencies" on the report and forward.
3. The income for the month for each property plus any delinquencies will equal the total monthly scheduled rents.
4. Under no circumstances will a delinquency be allowed for over 30 days. If tenant is over 30 days late, an eviction notice should be sent by certified mail with receipt requested to show proof of mailing. If the rent is over 15 days late, send out a seven-day notice to comply.

Expense Report

Property: _____ Date: _____
Prepared By: _____

AUTOMOBILE EXPENSES			MISCELLANEOUS		
Date	Item	Amount	Date	Item	Amount

Signed: _____ Date: _____
Approved By: _____ Date: _____

Instructions: Attach receipts to all automobile and miscellaneous expenses.

Individual Time Record

Property: _____ Date: _____

Prepared By: _____

Name:	Regular Hrs.
Employee Number:	Overtime Hrs.
Position:	Sick Hrs.
Pay Period Starting:	Vacation Hrs.
Pay Period Ending:	Commission $_____

Job #	1 16	2 17	3 18	4 19	5 20	6 21	7 22	8 23	9 24	10 25	11 26	12 27	13 28	14 29	15 30	31	Total

Comments:

_____

_____

_____

_____

_____

I hereby certify that the above hours are correct.

Employee's Signature: _____

Supervisor's Approval: _____

Instructions:
1. This report should be completed on a monthly basis.
2. Upon approval, the records will be submitted for disbursement.

Marketing Checklist

Property: _____   Date: _____

Prepared By: _____

	INITIAL	DATE	COMMENTS
OPERATING DATA ANALYSIS			
Tenant profile			
Traffic log			
Inspection report			
Social program			
CURRENT MARKETING INCENTIVES			
Current tenant (referral fee)			
Real estate broker (home finder fee)			
Noncompetitive manager (referral fee)			
Moving allowance			
On-site manager incentive			
Free rent (new tenant)			
Free rent (current tenant referral)			
Prepayment discount % (1 year)			
ADVERTISING/PROMOTION			
Local papers (newspapers)			
Directories			
Local advertising and news circulars			
Yellow Pages			
Brochures			
Radio/TV			
Direct mail			
Chamber of Commerce			
Billboards			
Associations			
MARKET SURVEY CONTENTS			
Competitive analysis			
Planning Commission information			
Chamber of Commerce information			
Bank personal comments			
Local real estate broker information			

Instructions:
1. This report is due on an as-needed basis.
2. Complete all information required on form. If not applicable, write N/A.
3. Once all information is gathered, write a narrative report that is to be attached to all materials. The report should include population trends, business growth, competitive projects, zoning, proposed new construction, etc. Also include any recommendations as to the existing market, program, capital expenditure required for project, rent increase and timing and projected project fill rate and cash flow.

Occupancy Report

Property: _____ Date: _____

Prepared By: _____

Size of Project (Total Units/Sq. Ft.): _____

LINE		NUMBER	PERCENT OF TOTAL
1	Occupied beginning of week/month—units/sq. ft.		
2	Plus moved in during period—units/sq. ft.		
3	Subtotal		
4	Minus moved out during period—units/sq. ft. Reasons for move-outs: _____ _____ _____		
5	Net at end of period (Sunday)—units/sq. ft.		
6	Leased beginning of week/month (deposit held)—units/sq. ft.		
7	Plus leased during period—units/sq. ft.		
8	Subtotal		
9	Minus refunds during period and/or move-ins on Line 2—units/sq. ft.		
10	Net leased end of period		

Instructions:
1. Prepare this report as required and send to home office.
2. Keep copy for file.
3. Detail reasons for move-out, whenever possible.
4. Percent of total is defined as number of units/sq. ft. rented divided by total size of project.

Petty Cash Recap

Property: _____   **Date:** _____

Prepared By: _____

DATE	PAY TO	DESCRIPTION	ACCOUNT NO.	AMOUNT		BALANCE ON HAND	
	TOTAL:						

Additional Bills (Attached): _____
_____
_____

Comments: _____
_____
_____

Instructions:
1. Petty cash will be replenished only if all columns of form are completed (except for Account No.).
2. Add back replenished amount in order to balance the last column (Balance On Hand).
3. Attach receipts for expenses to form before submitting to home office.

Tenant Roster — Commercial

Property: _____   Date: _____   Prepared By: _____

UNIT NO.	TENANT NAME	TYPE	AREA SQ. FT.	MONTHLY RENT	PER SQ. FT.	LEASE TERMS	LEASE DATE	COMMENCE DATE	TERMINATION DATE	COMMENTS
TOTALS:										

Instructions:
1. This report is due on an as-needed basis.
2. Keep one copy for on-site office files.
3. Sequence by unit number, not alphabetically.
4. Comments column should include any security deposits or CAM charge percentages.

Tenant Roster — Residential

Property: _____   Date: _____   Prepared By: _____

UNIT NO.	TENANT NAME *Property*	MONTHLY BASE RENT	UTILITIES	(OTHER CHARGES) *Insurance* *Tax*	*Other*	DEPOSITS *Date*	MOVE-IN DATE *Amount Paid*	LEASE TERM MONTH/YEAR *Interest*	COMMENTS *Balance*

Instructions:
1. This report is due on an as-needed basis.
2. Keep one copy for on-site office files.
3. Sequence by unit number, not alphabetically.

Tool and Equipment Inventory

Property: _____ Date: _____

Prepared By: _____

QUANTITY	ITEM/DESCRIPTION	CONDITION
	GROUND EQUIPMENT:	
	HAND TOOLS:	
	MISCELLANEOUS EQUIPMENT:	

QUANTITY	ITEM/DESCRIPTION	MANUFACTURER	MODEL SERIAL NO.	CONDITION
	OFFICE EQUIPMENT:			
	POWER EQUIPMENT:			

Instructions:
1. This report should be completed at least once a year.
2. A copy should be sent to the home office with any comments or requests for new equipment.

Utility Log

Property: _____   Date: _____

Tenant: _____   Unit No: _____

Utility Company: _____   Account No: _____

Date Meter Read	Meter Reading	Usage	Amount	Payment Date

Instructions: To be filled in every month when billing has been received from utility company. Bill tenant accordingly.

Index